WIN THE WAR WITH YOUR INNER CRITIC

UNDERSTANDING THE INNER CRITIC'S ROLE IN YOUR SUCCESS

MIKE McCAFFERTY, LPC, CPC

Win the War with Your Inner Critic: Understanding The Inner Critic's Role In Your Success
Published by MPM Publications, Denver, CO

ISBN: 978-0-578-85512-7

SELF-HELP / Personal Growth

Cover and page design by John McCafferty, McCafferty Advertising, LLC, Louisville, KY

QUANTITY PURCHASES: Schools, companies, professional groups, and other organizations may qualify for special terms when ordering quantities of this title.

For information, email mikemccaffertycoaching@gmail.com.

This book reflects the author's present recollections of experiences over time. In some instances, events have been compressed and dialogue has been recreated. The names and identifying characteristics of some persons described in the book have been changed.

PUBLICATIONS

This publication is meant as a source of valuable information for the reader/participant. However, it is not meant as a substitute for direct expert assistance. If such level of assistance is required, the services of a competent professional should be sought. Any self-help resource has both risks and benefits. The material in this video, book and companion workbook is intended for educational purposes only. No expressed or implied guarantee as to the effects of the use or recommendations can be given or liability taken by MPM Publications, Mike McCafferty Coaching, LLC or any affiliated individuals.

Acknowledgements

Both of my parents did a phenomenal job of raising eight children. Even though dad's parental instincts were sometimes misguided, his loving intentions were never in question. Caring for his family was one of his most important values. Those who knew him well vehemently agree. Many years after his passing, dad's legacy looms large in all of our lives, and mom remains a great family matriarch.

My dad was the greatest man I've ever had the privilege of knowing. I'm eternally grateful for both his greatness and his flaws. Today, I measure him by objective standards rather than the skewed portrayal my Inner Critic would have me believe. Living up to his legacy remains my greatest life challenge.

Whatever I accomplish in life, I attribute in large part to the efforts of both of my parents. As in the words of 12th century theologian John Salsbury, "We are like dwarfs sitting on the shoulders of giants." The lessons I've learned about life and myself are the result of my observations and interactions with my family, friends, colleagues, and clients. I used to think that it would be nice if all of my relationships were easy, but if that had been the case, I never would have understood the gifts that each challenge presented. I'm glad that we have persisted, because in the end, it has been well worth it. I look forward to many more lessons at the hands of the wonderful people I've been blessed to cross paths with over the years.

I hope that I can extend at least an approximation of the love and support my parents provided us, to my wife Shannon, our adult children, their spouses, and our current and future grandchildren: Michael Ben, Keria and Mikey; John Shannon and Laura; Hannah, aka Sugar Bear, Joshua and BBBB.

Table of Contents

COMPANION WORKBOOK

Please click this link to download the **FREE** Companion workbook for exercises 4, 5, 5 (Answers), 10, 12, 15, 17 and 18.

WinTheWarWithYourInnerCritic.com

Once you download the PDF, you can fill in and save the exercises on your computer or print the pages and fill out the exercises manually.

You will need Adobe Reader on your computer.
You can download it for FREE at https://get.adobe.com

Introduction

Few things are more upsetting than knowing someone has made it their life's mission to constantly belittle and bully you. They hold you back from achieving your full potential. To make matters worse, anything you do to get them off your back only emboldens them. They persist with their provocations until they achieve their desired end—your complete and total compliance.

You fight, beg, or even surrender in the hope that you can stop the onslaught, but regardless of the intensity of your efforts, they persist. Resistance only stiffens their resolve to control your thoughts and subsequent actions. The irony is, they're a creation of our own making, and we always carry them with us. They mislead and manipulate us into doing their bidding. In the words of a 1972 Pogo Comic Strip, "We have met the enemy, and it is us."

Our greatest foe is our own Inner Critic.

They arise from the interplay between significant individuals in our external environment and our interpretation of those interactions. Always on the prowl and in-tow, they'll assume various forms depending on our specific circumstances. They color our thoughts, our emotions, and our decisions. They're determined to keep us mired in a life of mediocrity by sowing seeds of doubt and discontent. They're shrewd adversaries and always know just the "right things" to say based on our current vulnerabilities.

At the outset of new projects, they make them more challenging by weighing us down with excessive emotional baggage and distractions. It's as if we're carrying an extra 100 pounds of dead weight. Right when we need our confidence most, they "remind" us that our previous successes were just lucky breaks rather than a result of our efforts.

When they're not minimizing and scorning our abilities or achievements altogether, they diminish them in comparison to others. They gnaw away at our sense of satisfaction for a job well-done, like a rat chewing on a loose electrical wire. They are the primary entity that holds us back from achieving significant goals. Their impact is incalculable. Until we develop productive responses, our options are usually limited to perpetual warfare or humiliating submission. There are two basic types of Inner Critic. The most common form, and my constant companion, is the **Type I: External Protector—Internal Dictator.** The second form is the **Type II: External Bully—Internal Dictator.** I'll elaborate on these concepts in chapter three.

Although the source and intentions are very different, both have strikingly similar manifestations and impact. While no one's completely immune from their influence, there is some good news. Conscious awareness allows us to anticipate their tactics and enact productive countermeasures to keep them at bay. This book describes the sequence of events that led to the revelation of my Inner Critic and his progression from birth through his[1] present-day manifestations. It depicts the insidious impact Inner Critics have on our lives and how society unwittingly nurtures the seeds that support their development. You'll learn to pause the tape in your head, recognize the lies, and replace them with more productive alternatives.

Practical exercises at the end of each chapter will allow you to renegotiate a more favorable relationship with your Inner Critic and tip the balance of power in your favor. You'll be amazed at what you (re)discover about yourself, and success, as you define it, will become your new normal.

IMPORTANT NOTE:

Please complete the exercises in the companion workbook in the same sequential order indicated in this book. Although each exercise is useful, the entire puzzle is greater than the sum of its parts. This will provide you with the best opportunity to, *Win the War Against Your Inner Critic*.

---

[1]My Inner Critic is the embodiment of my father's harsh messages and protective intentions. For that reason and for the sake of convenience and consistency, I use the pronouns "he," "him" or "it" to designate Inner Critics throughout this book. Your Inner Critic may be male, female or genderless.

SECTION ONE

SEEK FIRST TO UNDERSTAND . . .
YOURSELF

SECTION
TWO

CHAPTER ONE

GROUND ZERO:
ENTERING CONSCIOUS AWARENESS

More than four decades later, my first conscious experience with my own Inner Critic continues to resonate. Until the age of 25, I was completely unaware of "his" existence. It was only after a "Big Bang" encounter that I came face-to-face with my internal tormentor. Prior to that blinding realization, he spoke in subtle tones, and our encounters were far too fleeting for me to recognize. I was totally unaware of his presence, his lies, and his intentions.

At the time of this chance encounter, I was a therapist at an adolescent treatment facility in suburban Philadelphia. With more than five years in the field and a hard-won reputation as an excellent therapist, I had hit a glass ceiling. In order to advance my career, I'd have to earn an advanced degree.

I never seriously considered my colleagues' assertions that I was capable of such an accomplishment. I had barely squeaked by at the undergraduate level. In those four years, I earned a less-than-sparkling 2.3 grade point average. The two A's I earned were in "gimme classes" where the only requirement was to show up.

My family and friends questioned my hesitancy to enroll in graduate school, but I (in concert with my Inner Critic) consistently blew them off. After two years of lame excuses and foot-dragging, I reluctantly applied to Temple University's counseling program. To my great surprise, I was accepted. I secretly hoped they'd turn me down, so I could put the "ridiculous notion" of graduate school to rest. When I received my acceptance letter, my Inner Critic responded with sarcasm. He reminded me of a quote from Groucho Marx: "I never want to belong to any organization that would have me as a member."

He continued to reinforce my doubts with unconscious, denigrating messages that I only understood in retrospect. Those messages went something like this:

Whew. You really fooled those guys. . . . Temple must have lowered their standards. . . . Getting accepted is one thing, but completing grad school is another. . . . They'll catch their mistake soon enough. . . . C'mon Mike, anyone with half a brain can figure out that you're NOT suited for graduate school.

Ironically, the support of friends and colleagues just added to my angst. How could these people who had my best interests at heart be so wrong? Why didn't they support my false narrative of personal incompetence?

In the weeks prior to the start of class, my Inner Critic continued to pepper me with similar talking points. His negative drumbeat grew louder and more insistent with each passing day. For my part, I was an unsuspecting accomplice by latching onto those messages and repeating them over and over on a continuous loop. He also added a ridiculous stipulation designed to cause further hesitation and self-sabotage.

You'll never keep up if you take more than one course at a time, and if you earn anything less than an A, it will prove once and for all that you're incapable of completing the program.

Despite the absurdity of those sentiments, I believed his lies and acted accordingly. Having been groomed by my Inner Critic for many years to believe whatever he said as absolute fact, it never occurred to me that I could challenge his assertions. He's a cunning manipulator and con artist who couches ridiculous stipulations and distorted messages in language that makes them seem plausible.

I have often wondered how I could be so blind to my Inner Critic's tricks. Then I happened upon a story about con artists. Like a lot of people, I assumed the con in con artist stood for convict. I Googled the term and discovered that the "con" in con artist actually stands for confidence. In other words, con artists gain our confidence and then take advantage of our trust and vulnerabilities. Our Inner Critic is the ultimate con artist.

He had me convinced that earning anything less than an A would prove his point—that I was incapable of earning a graduate degree. To make matters worse, his incessant, negative chatter intensified whenever others challenged him. The tensions escalated to agonizing levels when my external reality (friends and family) and my internal reality (dominated by my Inner Critic) clashed over those discrepancies.

Colleagues were either oblivious or baffled by my lack of attention to obvious details and uncharacteristic missteps. Surely, they would have understood if they knew of the battles that raged inside my head. They seemed content to shrug their shoulders, go about their business, and chalk it up to me being me.

Setting high academic standards is a worthy endeavor, and even perfectionistic tendencies can be helpful at times. However, my Inner Critic set impossible benchmarks to discourage me from ever trying. Perfection as he defined it, was practically unattainable.

Why bother? You can't do it anyway.

When I fought past his objections and fell short of a goal, he was always there to mock my efforts.

Told ya! I knew you couldn't do it.

On the other hand, when I achieved a goal, he'd respond with something like, *Everyone gets lucky once in a while. Even a broken clock is right twice a day.* In other words, heads he wins tails I lose.

It Was Time to Face My Fear

Although classes met on Saturday mornings from 9:00 a.m. to noon, my feelings of impending doom were a constant presence throughout the week. I experienced a brief respite immediately following class that lasted through the Sunday football lineup. Football provided an opportunity to avoid emotional discomfort by immersing myself in temporary, pleasurable distractions.

Like clockwork, my Inner Critic reappeared every Monday morning when I woke to the sound of my alarm buzzing. The intensity of his presence grew stronger with each passing day. Most days were a blur. By Friday afternoon, my anxiety was through the roof. It was practically unbearable. I'd sweat profusely, fumble my words, and visibly shake. It always surprised me that colleagues didn't seem to notice the difference in my demeanor. I must have been a great actor, appearing so calm when behind the façade, I was a nervous wreck. I felt like I was alone in an untethered elevator, plummeting from the top floor of the Empire State Building. My anxiety reached its climax each Saturday morning. It was a terrifying and extremely exhausting experience and a recurring theme throughout the first semester.

One Saturday morning midway through the semester, I overslept. This was an exceptionally bad idea since classes were held at an off-campus site in downtown Philly. Parking spaces were at a premium and nearly impossible to find. If I arrived after 8:30 a.m. I'd be lucky to find a spot less than a half-mile from my destination. Thankfully, I was startled out of my slumber by the deafening sound of thunder. I threw on my jeans, snatched a T-shirt from the laundry basket, and rushed out into a torrential downpour.

I took my usual route along the East River Drive. As I approached the downtown area, I frantically checked and rechecked the analog clock on the dashboard of my blue Subaru hatchback. I was already half an hour late, and the storm continued to slow traffic to a crawl. I knew I'd never find a parking space and would be drenched by the time I made it to class. Immediately, my Inner Critic's chatter kicked in:

What are you thinking Mike? Are you crazy? C'mon skip class. It's only one week. You don't want to make a spectacle of yourself. You'll be waaaaay too late and soaking wet.

Instinctively and without hesitation, I made a sharp U-turn and headed home. I was immediately startled by a physical jolt to my sensibilities, as if I was struck by lightning. For the first time in my life, I became consciously aware of my Inner Critic as a separate entity. I pulled over and parked my car by the side of the road. I was confused by the dramatic shift from the overwhelming panic I felt on the way to class to the incredible sense of relief I experienced when I decided to give up and head home.

I took several minutes to reflect on the emotional shift and realized that earning a poor grade in this class would "prove" my Inner Critic right. It would add legitimacy to his claims that I wasn't deserving or capable of earning and advanced degree. I grabbed the steering wheel as hard as I could and unleashed a scream, "What the hell just happened?"

Like Ebenezer Scrooge in Dickens's A Christmas Carol, I saw my life in a tableau of past, present, and future possibilities—what was, what is, and what would be—if I allowed my Inner Critic to maintain control. I gave voice to my pent-up rage and shouted, "You dirty bastard. I don't care if I'm late or soaking wet. I'm gonna get my ass to class, and I mean NOW!"

I turned the car around, drove to school, and parked in the first open spot I could find. The hellacious thunderstorm continued to rage as I jogged a half mile to class. I was 90 minutes late. A trail of water followed in my wake as I made my way to the first empty seat. The sodden weight of my drenched clothes complimented the squishy sound of my saturated sneakers. The professor and students stared at me with a sort of humorous curiosity.

My efforts to remain inconspicuous went unnoticed. I must've looked like a scraggly, wet mutt shaking itself dry. Water flew everywhere. Despite the overwhelming physical and emotional discomfort, I had begun to take back my power. For the first time in my life, I had told my Inner Critic to "F*** off!"

After years of uncontested compliance, my Inner Critic had been lulled into a false sense of security. Trapped by his own overconfidence, he was completely blindsided when I stood up to him. He couldn't believe that I dared challenge his authority. He knew it was the dawn of a new era, and he was nervous about losing his grip on power.

Despite my newfound awareness, I remained convinced of his ridiculous, underlying stipulation.

*You **HAVE** to earn an A in this class or else you'll never succeed at graduate school.*

He convinced me that anything less than an A would be a harbinger of things to come. It would put an end to the "silly" notion of graduate school and provide my Inner Critic "proof" of what he'd proclaimed all along:

You'll never succeed at the graduate level.

After years of unconscious manipulations, I was finally in the driver's seat and could begin to steer my life in a whole new direction. My increased awareness of my Inner Critic's chatter was helpful but also distracting. Focusing on my studies proved a lot easier said than done. There was a mountain of homework, and he continued to distract me with various enticements designed to lure me away from it and set me up to fail.

You'll have plenty of time to study later. Right now, the game is on TV. You don't want to miss it.... You deserve a break, Mike; you've been working too hard.... You need to clean up in here before you can study.... You better call your parents. You don't want them upset with you.

Inner Critics dangle a variety of "shiny objects" in front of us to relieve the tension associated with our immediate discomfort. Those "shiny objects" can range from excessive consumption of drugs/alcohol to obsessive television viewing to compulsive gambling to overeating. What often begin as harmless diversions can evolve into full-blown addictions. Our Inner Critic encourages us to lose ourselves in the immediate pleasure of the distractions at the expense of achieving our goals.

Inner Critics have much in common with the Sirens[2] of ancient Greek Mythology. They often whisper in nearly inaudible tones that quietly, though effectively, find their way into our subconsciousness. Prior to conscious awareness of my Inner Critic and his tactics, his commentary was camouflaged in muffled tones and difficult to decipher. Conscious awareness of his presence allows me to hear him loud and clear. It's comparable to upgrading my telephone system. I used to have two paper cups connected by a string. Now I use a landline.

Despite my struggles, my increased awareness of my Inner Critic allowed me to persist and concentrate on my studies. In the end, I earned that A. I overcame my ambivalence and enrolled in a second class. Once again, my effort paid off. I earned another hard-fought A. With it, I equaled the total number of A's I'd earned in four years of undergraduate studies.

---

[2] Sirens are dangerous creatures in mythology who lured sailors with their enchanting music and singing voices to shipwreck them on the rocky coast of their island.

It was then that I was reminded of something a self-made multi-millionaire once said, "Making my first million was the hardest. After that, it became second nature." Once I realized I was able to earn good grades by exerting the necessary effort, academic success became my new normal.

A few months later, my wife and I moved to a small town in Kansas. We took over the management of a group home for adolescent boys. My professor graciously allowed me to complete my third course from a distance. I received confirmation of my grade shortly after we moved. This time I fell short, just as my Inner Critic had predicted. Rather than achieving perfection with another A, I "only" earned an A minus.

During a long-distance call with my parents, I shared my "disappointing" academic update. I was especially hesitant to tell dad. He was a former Marine Corps Master Sergeant and had always been tough on us kids, especially when it came to academics. I was convinced I would disappoint him AGAIN—even with an A minus. After a few seconds of hemming and hawing on the phone, I finally drummed up the courage and blurted out,

"Well dad, I got my grade."

"Oh yeah Mike?" he asked. "How'd ya do?"

"I didn't earn an A this time."

"So, what did you get?"

"I got an A minus."

I anticipated a disappointed tone and a response that would go something like this:

"Oh great, Mike! An A minus. Now you'll never be able to maintain a perfect 4.0 GPA, no matter how hard you try. If you had only exerted a tiny bit more effort, you could have turned that A minus into an A. Now it's too late. There are no do-overs. You can get 100 straight A's from now through eternity, but it'll never be the same. It might be a 3.999999 G.P.A. but you'll never again achieve a perfect 4.0. I guess it was just too much to ask."

My Inner Critic was my dad's determined understudy. He memorized and memorialized these sentiments perfectly. I held my breath in anticipation of my dad's inevitable condemnation. When I reluctantly expressed "my shame" at earning an A minus, I expected him to remind me of my other imperfections. Instead, for the second time in a matter of months, my emotional world was rocked again. Dad threw me a curve and said, "I'm proud of you son."

I still don't recall anything else from that conversation aside from the swirl of emotions that left me spinning in a surreal funnel. It was the best gift he could ever give me.

As my dad's voice trailed off into the background, I realized that he'd moved beyond his demeaning messages but remained true to his loving intentions.

More Pieces of the Puzzle Emerge...

With the growing awareness of my Inner Critic and his deceitful messages, I became determined to prove him wrong once and for all. Objective truths began to emerge as I realized I could—and did—earn two graduate degrees. In both cases, I earned straight A's, with the one "blot" on my record of that single A minus.

Messages that had been designed to distract and set me up to fail began to lose their power. My Inner Critic wanted me to place blame for my short-comings on my dad's shoulders. Doing so would absolve me of personal responsibility. However, it also meant that he was my excuse to remain stagnant and fall short of my full potential. I began to understand the interplay between my dad (and other external critics) and my Inner Critic. Growing up, my dad had no idea how his words influenced me. Nor did he understand the dramatic impact of the five simple words, "I'm proud of you son."

Those words continue to resonate with me more than twenty years after his death.

Summary

At the age of 25, I became consciously aware of the existence of my Inner Critic as a separate entity. Once the battle lines were drawn, I sensed his distress. Conscious awareness of my Inner Critic, combined with my hard-earned success in graduate school and a providential encounter with my dad, proved instrumental in forging a new path forward. It dramatically altered my internal landscape, which became evident in my external environment when I overcame various obstacles and earned my graduate degree.

My Inner Critic developed in response to my misinterpretation of my dad's well-intentioned messages. Those messages became the foundational beliefs that led to the creation of my Inner Critic. I also realized that I could reject my Inner Critic's messages as an obsolete legacy—if I was willing to pay the price. One question remained: did I have the courage to act on these revelations?

Exercise #1: Your Most Important Relationships

Quickly, without overthinking and before you read my comments below, identify your three most important relationships.

If you're like many people, your list does not include yourself. Our relationship with others is an outward reflection of our relationship with ourselves. This doesn't diminish the importance of outward relationships. Instead, it elevates the priority of your relationship with yourself.

Exercise #2: Determine Your Locus of Control

Locus of control is a concept developed by Julian B. Rotter in 1954. It's defined as the extent to which people believe they have power over events in their lives. Our specific locus of control exists on a continuum between two extremes. Persons with an internal locus of control believe they can influence life events and their potential outcomes. Those with an external locus of control blame outside forces for the events in their lives.

Click or go to the following link and complete the exercise and then resume reading where you left off.

TinyURL.com/LocusControlTest

There's always an intersection between our internal conversations and our external environment. Those who believe they're helpless to manage most aspects of their lives will remain victims of those beliefs and external circumstances. Where we place our locus of control (internally or externally) impacts the degree to which we're able to manage our Inner Critic.

We operate from a place of strength when we effectively manage our internal conversations. This allows us to increase our options, influence people and circumstances, and achieve mutually beneficial outcomes. Consider your results of this exercise carefully and reflect on the impact your locus of control has on the most significant aspects of your life.

Exercise #3: Is Your Locus of Control More Externally Focused? Really?

Is your ability to impact life's circumstances more dependent on internal or external factors? If you believe your success is primarily externally focused, this exercise will challenge that perspective. You may want to record it to follow along without having to read or memorize the steps.

Step #1: Close your eyes.

Step #2: Envision a person you dislike who's caused a **MILD** amount of physical or emotional harm to you or someone you love. **AVOID RELIVING HIGHLY EMOTIONAL OR TRAUMATIC EXPERIENCES!**

Step #3: Take a few minutes to view the situation in vivid detail, as if it's taking place right in front of you, right now.

Step #4: Take a moment to ratchet up the intensity of your emotions.

Step #5: Imagine waving a magic wand over the person who caused your discomfort and watch them evaporate, right before your eyes.

Step#6: Envision a warm glow engulfing your entire body. Imagine receiving a nice, reassuring hug from a close family member or friend. Feel any remaining pockets of tension melt away.

Step #7: Open your eyes and answer the following questions:

    a) Is the person who hurt you or your loved one actually present, or did you just imagine them to be with you?

    b) How did your body respond to your thoughts?

    c) Did you experience muscle tension, racing heartbeat, clenching of teeth, nervous stomach, sweating, etc.?

    d) Was the experience as upsetting as you imagined?

    e) Did you notice any reduction in your anxiety after waving the magic wand and receiving the reassuring hug?

Completing the exercise demonstrates your ability to control your thoughts and emotions. It reminds you that you can redesign your internal environment to your liking. Since thoughts and emotions always precede behavior, you can also learn to adjust them as well. Changing your behaviors to productively impact your external environment is only possible if you believe that you can actually do so.

Of course, the laws of physics and external constraints do place some limits on our ability to "control" things, but we can certainly learn to manage circumstances within those constraints. The truth is that you have greater control over your life and external circumstances than you may have previously believed.

We always envision potential outcomes before taking steps to make them a reality. Consider how you prepare for a job interview. You anticipate the best clothes to wear, the types of questions you'll be asked, etc. Although you can't foresee everything about the interview, you'll do your best to prepare, so you'll be at your best on the big day. In the same way, we can't control every external circumstance, but we can prime ourselves to achieve the best possible outcome within our control.

Moving Forward

At the conclusion of each chapter, I'll challenge you to identify one thing you'll implement that week, based on the chapter. At the beginning of subsequent chapters, I'll ask you to describe something you've implemented from the previous chapter. These are your calls to action.

Identify one thing you'll implement this week based on Chapter 1:

_____

_____

_____

_____

CHAPTER TWO

IS THE INNER CRITIC A UNIVERSAL EXPERIENCE?

Did you implement something you learned from the previous chapter? If so, briefly describe the experience.

_____

_____

_____

_____

If not, please reconsider doing it this week.

For fifteen years I battled my Inner Critic before realizing a seemingly obvious fact—I was not unique nor alone in my struggles. However, I didn't experience this blinding flash of the obvious until I witnessed another person come face-to-face with her own Inner Critic. In that moment, I realized that my Inner Critic had countless partners in crime. That chance meeting occurred when I stared into the tortured eyes of a young inmate at the Wyoming Women's Prison (WWC) in Lusk, Wyoming. Her name was Kris. At the time, I was the Clinical Director of the Intensive Treatment Unit (ITU). The ITU is a long-term treatment program designed to help inmates overcome serious drug addictions and related lifestyle issues.

For many inmates, obtaining parole was largely contingent upon completing the Intensive Treatment Program and earning a G.E.D. Over the course of nearly two years, Kris worked tirelessly to address her multitude of treatment concerns. I was convinced that she'd more than earned the opportunity to plead her case before the parole board. Obtaining her G.E.D. was the last significant box to be checked. She'd studied for long hours preparing for the tests.

To obtain a G.E.D., individuals are required to pass tests in five subject areas. Each test can be taken up to three times during any calendar year. To increase their odds of success, I recommended the inmates take the tests in September. This allowed them to retake them again if necessary, in October and November. If they still hadn't passed all five subject areas, they could redouble their study efforts through December and take them three more times beginning in January.

Kris was a beloved figure in our unit and within the prison at large. She had risen through the inmate ranks to assume a leadership role in the community. She was an inspirational role model for residents and staff alike. Kris had overcome many personal demons to embrace a more productive lifestyle.

Kris easily passed four of the five required exams the first time she tested. The only subject area she failed was math. Two more attempts also ended in failure. At the outset of the new year, she took advantage of her three new opportunities. Despite tutoring support and long hours of study, she continued to struggle and ultimately failed the math exam two more times. Her final attempt occurred one week prior to her scheduled parole board appearance. If she failed again, she'd have to wait another nine months before she'd have another crack at it. Without her diploma, earning parole was unlikely. It was almost certain that she'd have to serve out the remaining years of her sentence.

On the day of the exam, everyone in the ITU anxiously waited to hear her results. Immediately following lunch, the PA system crackled to life, and the warden gleefully announced, "Congratulations, Kris, you earned your G.E.D.!" A loud, spontaneous cheer erupted throughout the prison. I leapt to my feet to offer her my personal congratulations. I was surprised to learn she wasn't celebrating with others but had instead isolated herself in her cell. Another inmate said, "She's in her room, Mr. McCafferty, and she's inconsolable."

I was puzzled and asked, "What do you mean inconsolable?"

"She's in her room crying and refuses to come out."

When I approached Kris's pod, she was lying facedown on her bed, sobbing into her pillow.

"Kris, you did it! Your persistence paid off. You earned your G.E.D. This is great news!"

Between stuttering sobs, she tried to speak.

"I'm not so sure, Mr. McCafferty."

I gave her a minute to catch her breath before asking, "How can you say that Kris? You worked hard, and now, you earned it!"

She slowly raised her head from her pillow, drew a deep breath, and gave me a look I'll never forget. Fighting back her emotions, she responded in her typically eloquent manner,

"I told myself for so long that I'd never pass that damn math test. Now that I have, I have to confront all the other lies I've been telling myself for so long: I'm a bad mom; I deserve to be treated like dirt by men; and I'll always be a drug addict." With that, she threw herself back onto the bed and continued to sob.

A chill ran down my spine. I was stunned into silence as another piece of my puzzle fell into place. I suddenly realized that Kris had her own Inner Critic and had spent most her life wrestling with its distortions and outright lies. Prior to that incident, I'd lived with my head down, focusing on my own internal clashes. It was like residing in a remote silo in the middle of nowhere. I had no idea that others shared similar struggles with a captor of their own making. A deep feeling of kinship welled up inside, and I felt an overwhelming sense of compassion and empathy for this young woman.

After leading hundreds of individual and group sessions over the course of many years, I realized they all had one thing in common—the presence of an Inner Critic. I'm now convinced, more than ever, that it is a universal phenomenon. There may be differences in the specific messaging or the extent of the damage, but the existence of other Inner Critics is undeniable.

I encourage you to complete the exercises and incorporate the lessons into your daily life. It will provide momentum to turn the tide and Win the War with Your Inner Critic. This is your opportunity to invest in yourself. Incorporating these lessons into your daily life will empower you to gain dominion over your Inner Critic. They will allow you to access the power to achieve your most important goals and attain a greater degree of personal fulfillment.

Exercise #4:   *Complete Exercise #4 in your workbook.*

Exercise #5:   *Complete Exercise #5 in your workbook.*

Before I share the answers to the questionnaire (Exercise #5), here are a few comments to provide some context. If you found this exercise challenging, you're not alone. It's based on the Miller Analogies, a graduate entrance exam. It is purposely designed to be challenging. As I recall, I had to earn a minimum of 60 out of 100 correct answers to be accepted into Temple University's graduate counseling program. After two months of intensive preparation with a study guide, I earned a score of 64. Objectively speaking, a 64 out of 100 is an F. So, if you struggled with some of the questions, consider yourself in good company.

I can't overemphasize the importance of language. Our words, and the meaning we attribute to them, play a pivotal role in either supporting our Inner Critic or reclaiming our authority. When I first created the Analogy Questionnaire, I called it a quiz. I later changed the title from quiz to questionnaire after many participants became visibly anxious and said they felt they were being judged. Although the questions remained the same, that one, seemingly insignificant, change in wording had the power to alter their perspective. This demonstrates the power of language to alter our thoughts and our emotional states.

When I ask participants to share their initial impressions of the questionnaire, they typically offer one of four responses. These include some variation on the following themes:

1. "I'm stupid" (referring to themselves);

2. "You're stupid" (referring to me);

3. "This is stupid" (referring to the instrument); or

4. perhaps the most productive response, "Hmmmmmm. This is interesting."

I'm still holding out for the response I'd like to hear most, "Mike, this is the greatest instrument in the history of human history. You're a flipping genius!" I figured, that as long as I'm dreaming, I might as well go all in, right? Whenever I share my favored response, it usually elicits a chuckle, or at least a smile, further proving my point. The words we string together form the messages that become our thoughts, and our thoughts always precede our emotions.

When we use hyperbolic language to define the typical ups and downs of life, it's reflected in our overreactions. An inmate at the prison once described the minor inconvenience of a missed phone call as "horrible." Labeling that event as "horrible" elevated her emotional and behavioral responses. She rushed about the ITU raising her voice and frantically gesturing to everyone, whether they cared to listen or not. By mislabeling a relatively minor event as "horrible," she set the stage for a dramatic overreaction. Manage your thoughts, manage your emotions, and master your life.

In addition to hyperbolic language, using absolutes to describe ourselves or various situations leaves us with no room for disagreement or opportunity to change. When I tell myself things like "I can't do that," or "I'm no good at that," I give myself a built-in excuse to give up without even trying.

Exercise #5 Answers: *Review after completing Exercise #5 in your workbook.*

The first five questions are purposely designed to be straightforward to mimic how we develop and then follow familiar patterns. Beginning with Question #6, your patterned responses no longer fit the previous questions. Many people get frustrated when they have to rethink the way they answer the questions. This is the same in life—we often get frustrated when our old patterns don't work on new situations. However, applying old habits to new circumstances rarely works out well. Consider this example:

Let's say you and I met face-to-face, and you brought along a hammer. Confused, I gave you a puzzled look and asked, "I've never seen one of those. What's it for?" Puzzled at my response, you say, "It's a hammer Mike." You continue to demonstrate its many uses and go on to tell me, "I have another one at home. You can have this one." (I don't normally accept gifts from clients, but this is only a hypothetical case, so I think I'm safe). Within a few weeks, the hammer becomes my favorite tool, and I find many uses for it. Since I want to keep it with me, I place it in the trunk of my car.

A few weeks later, you're driving down the highway and notice me on the side of the road fixing a flat. You slowly approach my disabled vehicle to offer assistance. Then you laugh when you realize I'm using my hammer to change the tire. When you calmly suggest a more appropriate alternative, I respond with agitation, "No thanks. I know what I'm doing. My hammer never lets me down. I'll change my own tire."

Our habits can blind us to better options. Using a hammer to change a tire doesn't make it a bad tool. It works perfectly well when it's used for its intended purpose. Similarly, most people consider smoking cigarettes a bad habit, but why would anyone light up in the first place? It's likely because they wanted to fit in with peers, be cool, or calm their nerves. Initially, smoking achieves those goal(s). Over time, they repeat the behavior until it becomes a physically addicting habit. Only after smoking becomes a firmly entrenched pattern do they begin to recognize the serious health implications and refer to it as a "bad habit."

Few would dispute that smoking cigarettes is counterproductive to a healthy lifestyle, but referring to it as a "bad habit" is a fundamental, linguistic error. Those words, "bad habit," have serious emotional and behavioral consequences. It's the kind of language Inner Critics like because it allows them to beat us up, promote feelings of guilt, and denigrate us for doing something "bad." When we feel guilty or experience other uncomfortable emotions, we seek relief. So of course, smokers often light up again to relieve that discomfort. It becomes a vicious chain reaction. Smoke—feel guilty—beat themselves up—feel increased tension—relieve it by lighting up. Those patterns reinforce the messages that we're bad, stupid, worthless, etc., or that we lack the ability to manage challenging aspects of our lives.

A more accurate description of "bad habits" is to refer to them as **Misapplied Strengths.** Misapplied Strengths are habitual response patterns that once served a useful purpose. However, they are no longer productive under the current circumstances. Referring to "bad habits" as "Misapplied Strengths" reduces judgement and allows us to view situations through a more objective lens. It also allows us to operate from a place of strength rather than one of guilt and frustration.

A logical progression of events (as illustrated with the first five Analogy Questionnaire questions) lulls most people into the assumption that subsequent situations will automatically adhere to the established pattern. Their thought progression becomes their habitual response, or Modus Operandi (MO). Questions #6–11 illustrate what happens when situations change— they present greater challenges because they require a different approach. When addressing new circumstances in life, we can either adhere to the same patterns that worked in the past and fail, or we can rethink our firmly entrenched responses and search for novel solutions that are more effective.

It can be confusing, frustrating, or even anger-provoking when we're thrown offtrack and are forced to reconsider our firmly entrenched patterns. More extreme emotional reactions seem increasingly prevalent in our immediate-gratification society. We're conditioned to expect instant solutions and want things to follow preconceived patterns. We don't want to stop, think, and consider alternative perspectives. That requires time and effort, both of which seem to be in short supply.

Habits that develop through patterned responses often save time and energy, but they also limit our choices. They encourage tunnel vision and reduce our incentive to develop more creative alternatives. Living by the adage "If it ain't broke, don't fix it" is fine, as long as we avoid an unconscious overreliance on it. Rather than continue to run into a "brick wall," we might want to consider using a ladder. Perhaps our greatest personal challenge is to avoid the unconscious tendency to blindly repeat behaviors that worked in the past.

In 1969, management trainer Martin M. Broadwell described the process of learning a new skill model as "the four levels of teaching." [i] To illustrate this process, I'll describe how I learned to tie my shoes (well before the advent of Velcro!). Despite the discomfort inherent in that learning process, I worked through it and, eventually, learned the new skill. Here are the stages of my shoe-tying process, in accordance with Broadwell's theory:

Stage #1: Unconscious Incompetence: As an infant, it never occurred to me that I didn't know how to tie my shoes. My parents always did it for me. I was unconscious of my incompetence.

Stage #2. Conscious Incompetence: With the increased mobility of toddlerhood, my shoes would come untied several times a day. I repeatedly tried retying them, with little success. The result was a jumbled mess of knots. At this point, I was consciously aware of my incompetence.

Stage #3: Conscious Competence: After several hours of tedious practice, I finally learned to tie my own shoes without help. However, it still required thoughtful consideration for each little step along the way. Mom's patient and soothing demeanor was very helpful in this process. "Take the end of both strings, Mike, and make a giant X. Pull one string under the bridge and make a bow." After a few weeks, I could tie my shoes without having to repeat that tedious mental process. At that point, I moved beyond Step #3 and onto Stage #4: Unconscious Competence.

Stage #4: Unconscious Competence: At the final stage, my muscle memory kicked in, and tying my shoes became an unconscious act. Nowadays, I barely remember tying them. Once we achieve unconscious competence in anything, we continue and further reinforce and internalize that behavior because it works…until it doesn't. Then it becomes a Misapplied Strength.

All four possible answers for the final question (#11) are less than perfect. Wouldn't it be wonderful if every decision we made had a single, clear-cut answer with no discernable downsides? The reality, however, is that many times we're forced to choose between imperfect possibilities. This may leave us with doubts as to whether we could have made a better choice. Others, especially our Inner Critic, will likely disagree with whatever option we choose. We may be left with the equivalent discomfort of an emotional pebble that's permanently embedded on the inside of our shoe.

When there are no "perfect" answers, many people freeze in inaction and cede control of their decisions to others or to life circumstances. Others get caught up in a repetitive cycle where they continuously second-guess whatever decision they make. They replay every possible downside and unwittingly remain on their internal hamster wheel, providing the fuel that energizes their Inner Critic.

Sample Script for Identifying a Misapplied Strength:

When we refer to habits as "bad," we do ourselves a great disservice. Complete the next exercise to reframe and rename what you formerly referred to as a "bad habit" as your Misapplied Strength. This will also help short-circuit your Inner Critic's demeaning comments. The following example can serve as a guide:

Something I've Referred to as a "Bad Habit":
Overeating
Original Purpose of My Overeating:
To feel better in the aftermath of an upsetting event, I may consume a half gallon of Rocky Road ice cream. Eating it serves the immediate, intended purpose of momentarily distracting me from my discomfort.
Long-term, Unhealthy Emotional/Physical/Relational Consequences:
Later on, I'm often disgusted with myself. I slip on some sweatpants because they're the only thing that fits; I get sleepy, and I'm less inclined to exercise.
My Inner Critic's Demeaning Comments:
"God you're pathetic."
"You're such a pig."
"No sense in exercising today."

Question #1: How do I describe my emotions in the aftermath of my Inner Critic's tongue-lashing? e.g., I'm sad, frustrated, and feel somewhat hopeless.

Question #2: How do these upsetting emotions increase or reduce the likelihood that I'll resort to the same quick fix? e.g., As a result of my sadness, frustration, and sense of hopelessness, I'm much more likely to seek comfort in another quart of ice cream. I'm also less motivated to engage in healthier alternatives that don't provide that immediate "fix." Avoiding healthier alternatives often leads to more emotional overeating and spirals into further weight gain. The more weight I gain, the more my Inner Critic kicks in to demean me, and the less motivated I am to engage in more productive alternatives.

Conclusion: Overeating was never a "bad habit." Initially it served the purpose of temporarily alleviating my discomfort. However, the long-term costs far outweighed its original benefits. This is another example of a Misapplied Strength. In time, I replaced that behavior with more productive alternatives. These included taking a hot bath, exercising, or meditating.

Now it's your turn.

Exercise #6: *Complete Exercise #6 in your workbook.*

Summary

Our natural tendency is to respond to routine situations in patterned, habitual ways. When confronted with novel events where our habitual responses no longer "work," we often get frustrated or even angry. We also experience some level of emotional discomfort when we are determined to find a perfect answer. Some people give up easily to avoid the emotional discomfort of stepping outside the safe confines of their comfort zone.

Many people become ensnared in a repetitive cycle where they latch onto self-doubts. They feed their Inner Critic additional ammunition to keep them stuck in a downward, self-defeating spiral. Still others become acclimated to their discomfort and accept it as a fact of life. Viewing novel situations with curiosity rather than judgement builds emotional muscle. It allows us to press the pause button and increases our ability to consider a range of alternatives before finalizing our decisions.

Identify one thing you'll implement this week based on Chapter 2:

_____

_____

_____

_____

SECTION TWO

INNER CRITIC GENESIS

CHAPTER THREE

FROM HUMBLE BEGINNINGS

Did you implement something you learned from the previous chapter?
If so, briefly describe the experience:

_____

_____

_____

_____

If not, please reconsider doing it this week.

Type I Inner Critic: External Protector—Internal Dictator

My theory regarding the origination of most Inner Critics crystalized during an interaction with my young grandson, Mikey. During a visit, I asked him, "What've you been up to buddy?"

He said, "Mom taught me how to ride my new bike." "Oh yeah? How'd it go?" He said, "She got really mad and yelled at me."

This is out of character for Keria, my daughter-in-law, so I asked, "What'd she yell at you about?"

He was nearly brought to tears when he told me, "Mom yelled, 'Look out Mikey. You're gonna get hit by that car!'"

Hmmm. I smiled because I understood his disconnect. Obviously, he'd misinterpreted intensity born out of love with angry disapproval. I explained the difference in language a seven-year-old could understand, and he seemed relieved. He gave me a hug, and we enjoyed the rest of our day. So, what does this have to do with the birth of most Inner Critics?

Well, Type I Inner Critics develop in response to seemingly innocent interactions between adult caretakers and their children. Both parent and child are innocent victims. They unwittingly engage in an interdependent dance. It culminates in the formation of the child's Inner Critic. As in the case of my grandson, these Inner Critics emerge in response to the child's misinterpretation of protective, parental interactions.

Infant Perspective:

Healthy parental interactions are on full display immediately following the birth of a newborn child. When loving parents return home with their bundle of joy, they're eager to protect and nurture it. However, conceiving a child is much easier than raising one, and infants can be exhausting. At the end of another long day, loving though weary parents reluctantly place the newborn into the crib for the night. A few hours later, they're awakened by the sound of screams. They jump out of bed and run to its aid. It's highly unlikely that they'd rush to the nursery and actually expect a verbal response when they ask, "What's the matter honey?"

It would certainly help if infants could offer a coherent verbal response. If so, they might respond with something like, "Well mom/dad, I believe my diaper is soiled. Would you mind looking into the matter? I certainly don't want to deal with an unpleasant rash. Besides, it's starting to stink in here."

To which parents would cheerfully respond, "Why certainly, Sugar. Thank goodness you didn't make us guess."

Instead, they quickly scoop the child into their arms, run through their mental Rolodex to determine the source of distress. They gladly play mind readers and guess until they figure out the answer to this riddle.

"Hungry?"

"Need a diaper change?"

"Too hot or too cold?"

"Just missing mommy?"

Once they address the source of the discomfort, the howling subsides. The baby falls asleep, and parents return to the comfort of their bed. Similar scenarios play out several times a night in millions of households all across the world. During infancy, children are masters of their domain. They appear to be helpless, but as long as their lungs work, they can keep their loyal subjects at the ready to address their every whim. This predictable response becomes an ingrained pattern. Infants lead; parents follow. Once the dance ends, the adults disappear out of sight. They only reappear when the infant rings the "servant's bell."

Infants in the nursery grow accustomed to this illusion and naturally assume it will remain that way forever. However, they're in for a rude awakening when their universe expands beyond the nursery. The abrupt and dramatic changes that occur when they enter toddlerhood are confusing and extremely frustrating. They never realized that the soft toys were carefully selected for the nursery. Now they expect to "play" with the new "toys" that lurk in plain sight just outside the prison bars of their playpens.

Electrical outlets, knives, and even the temperamental family pet can be hazardous to their health. They might as well be thinking, "My parents used to be my servants. They did my bidding without question. Now they're my adversaries. They prevent me from reigning over my kingdom."

The objective meaning of protective caretaker intentions are just that— to protect the child. However, the toddler's misinterpretation forms the basis for their fundamental disconnect. Screaming their heads off used to be a foolproof measure for getting what they want, so it's disconcerting when the winds of change sweep across their landscape. Sympathetic big people no longer drop what they're doing and give them what they want.

"When I was hungry, I screamed and got fed."

"When my diaper needed changing, I screamed and got changed."

"When I was sad or lonely, I screamed and got picked up and reassured."

The abrupt shift from their previous lives as infants is incomprehensible. In this brave new world of toddlerhood, they're forced to confront this more restrictive reality.

Toddler Perspectives:

Toddlers are naturally curious. When they leave the nursery, they want to investigate everything in their ever-expanding universe. Part of their exploration process is to imitate the behaviors of older siblings and adults. Since they view themselves as invulnerable, they fail to recognize the potential hazards when left to their own devices. Unless they're closely supervised, they can hurt themselves. Understandably, they're indignant when their parents' protective instincts clash with their curiosity and newfound mobility.

Now, their parents rush in and remove hazardous objects and the family pet. Rather than bending to their child's will and handing forbidden items over to them, they chastise the child for going near them. Most toddlers tend to fall into one of two general categories. Of course, there are some overlaps and exceptions, but most exhibit the basic characteristics of one category or the other. I refer to them as Determined Toddlers and Easygoing Toddlers.

Determined Toddlers present a greater, immediate challenge since they're unwilling to accept the world as adults tell them it is. They insist on investigating it for themselves. Easygoing Toddlers tend to be more compliant and require less parental attention. As in most cases, the squeaky wheel (Determined Toddler) gets the grease. Easygoing Toddlers just keep rolling along and appear to be doing just fine on their own.

Determined Toddlers view their parents' actions as punitive whenever they're barred from accessing the things they want. They become even more determined to "play" with the forbidden objects. When denied access, they throw tantrums and get into mischief. Their defiance becomes even more pronounced when they enter the "terrible twos." Parents become increasingly frustrated, and for the sake of the child, take more restrictive measures. They become embroiled in a perpetual arms race. Determined Toddlers strain to escape their shackles, and frustrated adults resort to increased urgency and intensity.

Determined Toddlers wonder, "Why does everyone else get to do all that cool stuff while I'm forced to watch from this stupid playpen, child restraint seat, shopping cart, etc.? I should be able to play with that electric socket or brush the dog's face too."

Parents counter with, "No! No! Don't touch that!" or "That's bad!" or "You're not old enough."

Consistent parenting is a time-consuming and challenging endeavor. It's especially difficult with the increased prevalence of single-parent households. However, as former British Prime Minister Neville Chamberlain learned when he tried to appease Adolf Hitler, giving into a bully to achieve "peace in our time" (by giving him a piece of another country without their consent) results in an inevitable long-term, catastrophic war. Whether "the bullies" are evil individuals like Adolf Hitler or Determined Toddlers, giving in to unreasonable demands reinforces their sense of entitlement and increases their appetite for immediate gratification.

They cling to their belief that they can "force" others to give in to their demands by raising hell. "I'll just scream until they give me what I want."

When parents stay the course and refuse to capitulate, Determined Toddlers proceed to scream even louder. Eventually, they fall asleep or become distracted with something else. Parents might assume that Determined Toddlers will abandon their efforts to brush the dog's face with a wire brush, but that illusion only lasts as long as parents are in the room.

Determined Toddlers' unconscious thought process goes something like this, "First I'll point and whine. If they don't give me what I want, I'll scream until they do . . . or I'll get it myself as soon as they leave. Where'd they hide that damn dog brush?"

The immature toddler brain misinterprets benevolent intentions designed to protect them as seemingly harsh messages. When they hear, "That's bad!" they internalize those messages as indication that they are "bad" and that trying new things is dangerous and should be avoided.

Although they're more compliant, Easygoing Toddlers internalize some of those same messages a bit different from their more strong-willed counterparts. Rather than fighting protective restrictions, they tend to go along with them. They internalize those restrictions as reflections of their own ineptitude. They follow carefully prescribed paths laid out by their parents or other "all-knowing adults." This tends to squash their self-reliance and constrain their creativity. They learn to accept their own perceived incompetence as objective fact.

The Easygoing Toddler is deceptively calm and accepting of these restrictions. When they reach for the glass pitcher and are scolded, they internalize the harsh messages and fail to recognize the protective intentions. Their thought processes go something like this:

"Everyone else must be smarter than me. I wish I was that smart."

The balance of power remains squarely with the parents and is rarely challenged. They're convinced of their parent's infallibility and comply with parental wishes because they believe that resistance is futile. So why bother? Parents appreciate their compliance and shower them with praise, hugs, and other rewards.

"You're such a good boy... Here's a lollipop for playing nicely in your playpen... Mommy loves her well-behaved little guy."

Easygoing Toddlers learn that compliance is good. Quietly playing with a wooden spoon all afternoon while parents get their work done makes mummy and daddy happy, and I get candy. Easygoing Toddlers are likely to give up without a fight. It's as if they shrug their shoulders and tell themselves, "Who needs to brush the dog's face anyway?"

These types of interactions, repeated over time, form the basis for Type I Inner Critics. Raising healthy children requires, fair, firm, and consistent discipline where they get a voice but not a vote. Regardless of whether the toddler is more determined or easygoing, they reflexively reinforce those original distorted messages on a continuous loop. This continues throughout their lives. When external critics aren't pointing out their mistakes, their Inner Critic gladly steps in to fill the void. It doesn't matter whether their missteps are real or imagined because their Inner Critic chastises them as if they're always objectively true. Some people envision their Inner Critic as a separate being. However, others perceive it as a disembodied, disapproving voice.

When someone refers to themselves as their own worst critic, they're absolutely right. Many proclaim it as if it's a medal of honor they proudly display. They've spent years allowing their Inner Critic to seize, intensify, misinterpret, reject, or twist events or messages until they conform with their preconceived narrative of their unworthiness. They spend a lifetime reinforcing those distorted mantras that reconfirm their incompetence. Practice makes perfect, right?

There can be many underlying motivations for demeaning self-statements. They can range from an overzealous religious impulse to keep themselves humble to misguided efforts to push themselves toward impossible standards of perfection or to elicit pity and reassurance from others. Here's an example of how this works. When someone tells them:

#1: *"You're really dumb."*

They take comments like this seriously and even intensify them when they're said in jest.

Inner Critic Translation: *He's right. That was a dumb mistake. I am dumb. . . . Yeah, he said he was just kidding, but I know he really means it. I am dumb.*

#2: *"Good job, Mike!"*

Inner Critic Translation: *He always says that. You know he doesn't mean it. I'm sure someone else could do better. You're not really that smart. It was just a lucky break.*

#3: *"Okay Mike, we'll go with your plan."*

Inner Critic Translation: *Geez, I wonder what she meant by that? She sure sounded hesitant. She's probably just saying that to make me feel good. I'm sure she thinks someone else has a better idea.*

For these folks, every comment enters a perceptual funnel similar to flies falling into an inescapable trap. Over the course of their lives, the number of truly critical comments (or those internally translated as such) tend to far outnumber the uplifting and supportive ones they receive from others.

Type II Inner Critic: External Bully—Internal Dictator
Many people understandably assume that Inner Critics originate in response to abusive life experiences. However, it's more likely that they begin as Type I: External Protectors and are later overtaken by subsequent bullying experiences. In these cases, the Inner Critic evolves into Type II: External Bully or some combination of both.

In the case of the Type II Inner Critic, conscious awareness of the Type I Inner Critic recedes into a person's subconscious when subsequent, more strident bullies take center stage. Most External Bully—Internal Dictators disguise the true underlying nature of their Inner Critic. The process is comparable to driving 500 miles down a long, desolate highway. There's nothing much to see until you drive past a horrific car crash. The rubber-neckers slow traffic to a crawl, even after the EMTs and police remove most of the wreckage. As you continue down the highway, the accident becomes a distant memory in the rearview mirror. Later, when asked about your trip, the first thing you mention is the accident. You largely forget that most of it was boringly routine and uneventful.

While most people readily recall memorable bullying events (as embodied in their Type II: External Bully—Internal Critic), they tend to forget the untold number of routine interactions with protective caretakers over the course of many years.

There are, however, rare instances when an External Bully is the original inspiration for an Inner Critic. My first awareness of this variation occurred when I worked with a young woman named Kelsie. (Like Kris from the women's prison, I altered her name to protect her privacy.) When we discussed her upbringing, it was apparent that, unlike the vast majority of us, Kelsie's Inner Critic arrived before she was a toddler, and the Type II Inner Critic had the opportunity to sink its talons into her.

When Kelsie was a newborn and brought home from the hospital for the first time, her older sister, Casey, viewed her as an imminent threat. When-ever they were away from the watchful eyes of their parents, a very jealous and vindictive Casey pinched, slapped, and called Kelsie names. The recurring events were enough to emotionally traumatize Kelsie but not enough to leave a mark or get Casey into trouble with their parents.

"You're stupid. You're ugly. Nobody will ever love you. You never do anything right."

Before Kelsie's arrival, Casey maintained a monopoly on their parent's affections, and she viewed Kelsie as an interloper. Like many older siblings who crave the same level of attention they received from parents when they were younger, a new addition can usurp that favored child status. It's hard not to be jealous of all the "oohs and aahs" that are bestowed on the newcomer. In the view of the older sibling, there's no room to share the spotlight. As the years passed, the harshness of Casey's demeaning comments and bullying tactics increased in direct proportion to the perceived threat. They remained a constant presence.

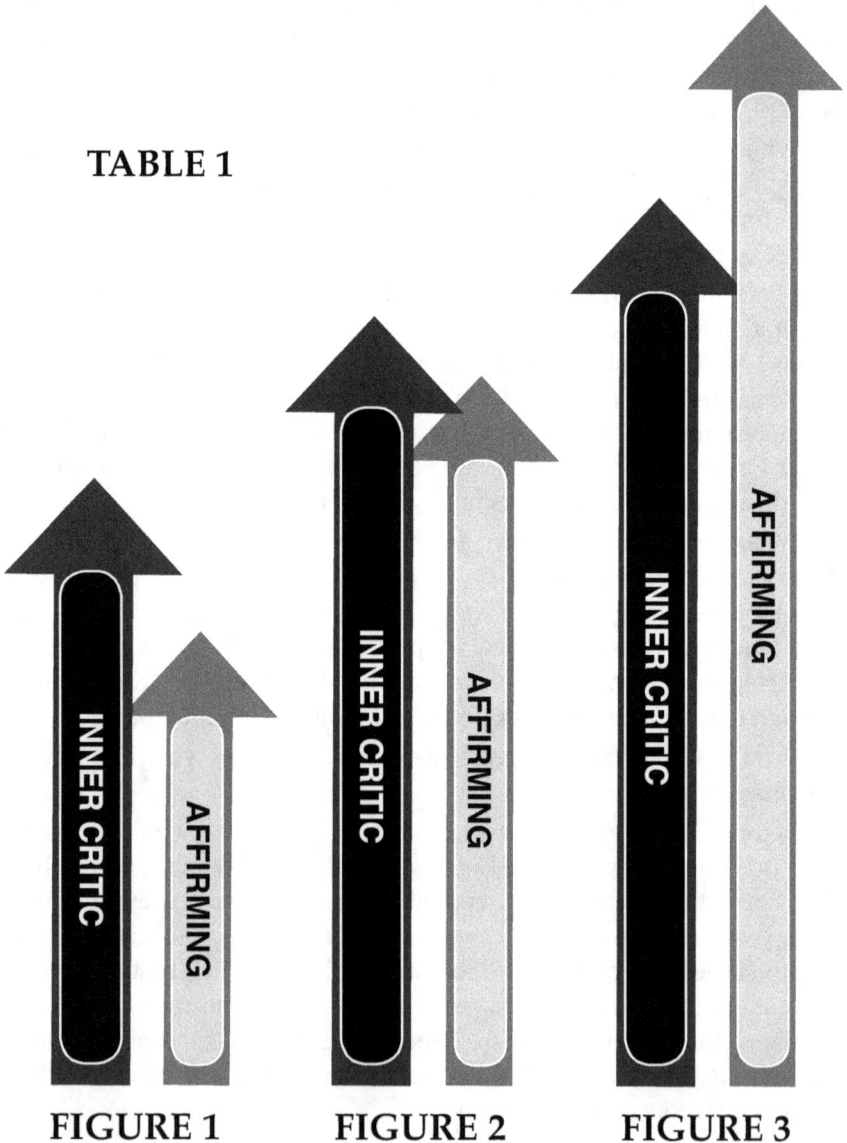

Similarly, other instances of the Type II Inner Critic as the primary presence occurs when a young child has the unfortunate experience of being born into an abusive and neglectful environment that continues throughout their childhood. The parental figures are unwilling or incapable of giving them the loving, protective foundation that (hopefully) most children are born into. Like Kelsie, these early childhood experiences lay the foundation for the development of their Type II Inner Critic: External Bully—Internal Dictator.

TABLE 1

INNER CRITIC

AFFIRMING

INNER CRITIC

AFFIRMING

INNER CRITIC

AFFIRMING

FIGURE 1   **FIGURE 2**   **FIGURE 3**

Understanding the intentions and messaging of our specific Inner Critic(s) allows us to devise the tools we need to address them in more productive ways. In the case of Type I Inner Critic: External Protector—Internal Dictator, the idea is to reject the message and embrace the intention. For Type II Inner Critics: External Bully — Internal Dictator, the message and intentions are the same. In these cases, reject both — the message and the intentions.

Table 1 includes three sets of parallel towers. The Inner Critic Towers represent the demeaning messages that bombard us from external sources that we subsequently replicate and reinforce within. Inner Critic Towers are like sheets of fly paper. Demeaning messages stick and reinforce our narrative of unworthiness. The Affirming Towers represent the productive messages we receive from external sources or generate internally. Unlike the fly paper on the outside of the Inner Critic Towers, the Affirming Towers are coated with Teflon, so constructive comments easily slip off and fall to the wayside.

Until we develop effective countermeasures, demeaning comments will continue to stick and become a prominent feature in our internal environment. It's our Inner Critic's "gift that keeps on giving." We can learn to deflect demeaning messages rather than allowing them to stick and weigh us down as they accumulate over time.

The Starting Gate

Regardless of when we become aware of our Inner Critic and its devious tactics, our Inner Critic Tower always has a huge head start. Catching up and surpassing it is only possible if we understand the rules of the game and then use them to our advantage. If not, our Inner Critic will remain the dominant force in our internal conversations and continue to torment and distract us from achieving our full potential. Without decisive action, the discrepancy between the two towers will continue to accelerate in our Inner Critic's favor. However, we can remove some of the fly paper and make it more difficult for demeaning messages to stick. The tools I describe also provide ways to replace the Teflon coating on your Affirming Tower with fly paper to make it easier for supportive comments to stick.

The Inner Critic Tower in Figure 1 in Table 1 is much taller in comparison to the Affirming Tower. It represents the head start our Inner Critic has at the dawn of our conscious awareness of its existence. Figure 2 shows the dramatic shift in comparative rates of growth after we enact effective countermeasures. Although it's impossible to remove all traces of our Inner Critic's presence from our psyche, we can shift the balance of power in our favor.

With targeted effort over time, more productive messages will overtake the derogatory chatter and outperform your Inner Critic's messaging, as indicated in Figure 3. Once the balance of power shifts in your favor, the impact of your constructive, internal conversations will continue to accelerate faster than the demeaning commentary. As this happens, your instinctive thoughts and responses will automatically focus on productive alternatives. Meanwhile, your Inner Critic chatter will be increasingly relegated to background noise.

The Relationship Between Labeling and Our Inner Critic

Labeling Theory[ii] explains how the identity and behavior of people are influenced by how others categorize or label them. Regardless of the source of the label (external or internal), giving it any degree of credibility shapes how we view and project ourselves to the rest of the world. If we believe a label to be true, it is true—at least for us.

The meaning we attach to labels can also change over time. When I was a young boy, people who wore glasses were derisively referred to as "four eyes." More recently, glasses have become a hip fashion accessory. Many people even wear glasses without prescription lenses because they believe they enhance their looks. In the same way, internalizing labels about ourselves either limits or expands the boundaries of what we perceive as possible. If I believe "I'm no good with numbers," then I have a built-in excuse for failing to balance my checkbook. Accepting derogatory labels as true provides fodder for our Inner Critic, who will ensure we confine ourselves to the limits of those boundaries.

Mislabeling

When our son, John, entered middle school, he tried out for the wrestling team. By the end of the first season, it was apparent that his talents were better suited for other endeavors. There was only one other wrestler that John pinned with regularity. That young man was the stereotypical chubby kid who chomped on candy bars during practice. He seemed unconcerned about the chocolate ring that was a permanent fixture around his mouth.

John internalized his losses as a reflection of his lack of talent and decided to quit the team at the end of the season. The following year, that same candy-bar-chomping, chubby kid became a state champion. After a little investigating, I discovered some interesting things about that young man. It turned out that he was third in a line of brothers who preceded him as wrestling champions. The two older siblings took him under their wings and explained that wins and losses were irrelevant during his first year. Instead, the first year was just an opportunity to observe others and learn the art of wrestling while training under the watchful eye of mentors. They taught him to view his lopsided losses as part of the process on the road to becoming a champion.

I'm not suggesting that John would have necessarily become state champion if he remained on the team, but it did leave me wondering: how much did his mislabeling of these events impact his wrestling experience? When labels become our reality, others join in and further reinforce them. The funny thing about labels is that they can originate from true, partially true, or completely untrue statements. Whether or not they're valid is irrelevant. The only thing that matters is whether we BELIEVE they are true.

Enacting effective countermeasures to challenge our assumptions allows us to engage in more productive conversations with others and our ever-present Inner Critic. To paraphrase the philosopher James Allen, our minds are like a garden. We can intelligently cultivate beautiful flowers or allow them to run wild with weeds.

Regardless of where, when, or how your Inner Critic originated, the impact on your emotional well-being is undeniable. It's much easier to build fortifications to block or contain your Inner Critic than to try to evict it from the premises after it's gained a foothold. Recognizing the precursors of your Inner Critic's arrival and then responding to its intrusion with effective countermeasures allows you to minimize or even sidestep its insidious tactics.

Exercise #7: *Challenge Your Inner Critic's Contempt with Curiosity*

Inner Critics speak with "the voice of authority," but even the world's greatest experts have made serious mistakes. Just a few short months before the Wright Brothers took off on their historic flight at Kitty Hawk, a top scientist published a report stating that heavier than air flying machines would never be practical.

How many "truths" that we "learned" and routinely accept as true turn out to be false? How many people gained weight by religiously following the food pyramid that was erroneously promoted by the U.S. Department of Agriculture? Prior to 1954, the scientific consensus was that running a mile in under four minutes was a physical impossibility. Since Roger Bannister broke that mark, it's been broken more than a thousand times.

Obviously, the four-minute mile was more a psychological barrier than a physical one.

On the other side of the coin is the fact that truth doesn't always gain acceptance and may even be scorned and punished. The great astronomer Galileo spent the last 30 years of his life on house arrest because he taught that the earth revolves around the sun. This factual science was suppressed because it failed to support the current religious doctrine of the time. Today, Galileo is heralded as a great astronomer, though few know the cost he paid for telling the truth.

Are your Inner Critic's messages always true? Are they consistent with the opinions of those who have your best interests at heart? What truths have you accepted as lies, and what lies have you accepted as truths? Challenge Inner Critic's messages like:

You're too old to . . . You're not smart enough to . . .

or any other statements designed to increase your self-doubts. You might pose questions like:

"Who are YOU to decide whether or not I'm too old? Or not smart enough? Just because I don't know of anyone who's done it, why can't I be a trailblazer and set a new standard?"

Ultimately, whether you decide to move forward on a particular project, it's your decision! Challenging Inner Critic's statements with curiosity demonstrates your unwillingness to reflexively yield to its commands without proper examination.

Exercise #8: *Use Affirmations*
"I am the greatest; I said that even before I knew I was."
—Muhammed Ali

Affirmations are powerful cognitive tools anyone can use to produce desired behavioral changes. From time to time, we all use affirmations without realizing it. Making it a regular, conscious practice allows us to override negative thought patterns and insert more productive ones. There are wonderful free or low-cost online resources and books that include affirmations you can adapt to fit your specific tastes. Here are several tips to consider when designing your own affirmations:

1. Keep them short. Repeat and focus on one message at a time. For example, I designed "I'm high and alive at 175" to help me achieve my ideal weight. Rhyming also makes them easier to remember. If your affirmations are long, I suggest you break them up into shorter ones.

2. **State affirmations in the present tense.** Rather than, "I want to be..." state your affirmation as if the desired state already exists, "I am..." You may notice a twinge of discomfort when you say something that's objectively untrue in the present tense. Persist despite the discomfort! It's just your Inner Critic's attempts to dissuade you from practicing because it challenges its commentary.

3. **State affirmations in positive terms.** Identify what you want rather than what you want to avoid. Telling yourself, "Don't think of a pink elephant," will probably conjure up a vision of a pink elephant. If you tell yourself, "Think of a blue rhinoceros," it's unlikely you'll think of a pink elephant.

4. **Feel your energy surge** as you state your affirmations to cheer yourself on.

5. **Construct several variations of the same theme.** For example, I might make three or four affirmations around the goal of healthy weight. "I'm high and alive at 175," "I am a mindful eater," "I eat to live rather than live to eat," etc. This allows me to use them interchangeably, and it keeps them fresh and less likely to get stale.

6. **Repeat affirmations throughout the course of the day.** You might put a sticky note on your steering column, bathroom mirror, computer screen, etc. These little reminders make effective and efficient use of your private moments.

7. **Choose one affirmation to repeat five or ten times in a row.**

8. **Download or record your affirmations to play back** when you're walking, driving, exercising, etc.

9. **Allow distractions to float away.** As in meditation, if something serves as a momentary distraction, allow it to float away rather than fight it. Fighting only increases its intensity. It's like trying to crush a rock in your shoe by stomping on it. If something is truly urgent, take care of it and then return to your affirmations.

10. **Briefly celebrate whenever you practice your affirmations.** As with physical workouts, results take time. Frame any discomfort as progress rather than an excuse to quit.

Exercise #9: *Use Visualizations*

Michelangelo said he created his famous statue of David, by "seeing an angel in the marble and carv[ing] until I set him free." His mental preview established a visual goal well before he put chisel to stone. We stimulate our subconscious to work toward the achievement of our goals when we do the same.

As with affirmations, many of us visualize without realizing it. We typically do so when preparing for a job interview, asking someone on a date, or planning how to behave when meeting a love interest's parents. Anticipating a desired outcome and picturing it in your mind's eye allows you to mentally preview that event in a positive light.

Here's my take on visualizations:

Step #1: Find a quiet, relaxing place where you can be undisturbed.

Step #2: Close your eyes, take five deep breaths, and exhale completely.

Step #3: Progressively tighten and relax your major muscle groups, working your way up from your feet.

Step #4: Imagine you're looking at a fuzzy TV screen. As you adjust the contrast, a significant goal comes into clear focus. It could be a job, a dream vacation, etc.

Step #5: Emphasize the pleasurable sensory aspects of your experience, including the sights, sounds, smells, tastes, physical sensations, and emotions. Become absorbed in the image of your desired outcome.

Step #6: Practice regularly. The more often you practice, the sooner you're likely to realize your desired results.

Summary

The original source of our Inner Critics usually originates from an External Protector where a child confuses adult caretaker intentions with their messages. Less common, but just as dangerous, are the Inner Critics that originate from an External Bully that acts out of their own insecurities. In either case, their emotional footprint remains a permanent and potentially powerful fixture in our internal landscape. Inner Critics far outlive the actual encounters that gave birth to them. It's like a relay race. External Protectors or Bullies pass the baton (demeaning messages) to our Inner

Critic, who keeps them in hand and runs with ever-increasing intensity. When we internalize these demeaning messages, our Inner Critics' immortality is ensured, even after the person who inspired them is no longer in our lives.

Once we're aware of our Inner Critic's existence, we can reject its messages, intentions, or both. Affirmations and visualizations are particularly effective in promoting desired outcomes. They can energize our emotions and establish new blueprints for safely addressing our Inner Critic. They allow us to challenge its demeaning messages from a proactive perspective. In the words of Psychologist Denis Waitley, "When you're without, do within."

A Brief Introduction to Chapters 4 and 5

In the chapters that follow, I'll introduce and expand on the concept of Emotional Fibromyalgia (EF), its connection with our Inner Critic, and how they work in concert to limit our success. I'll also illustrate how many common elements of modern American society wittingly or unwittingly reinforce our naturally occurring EF.

Identify one thing you'll implement this week based on Chapter 3:

SECTION THREE

INTERNAL AND EXTERNAL
WORLDS COLLIDE

CHAPTER FOUR

EMOTIONAL FIBROMYALGIA: A PETRI DISH FOR CULTIVATING OUR INNER CRITIC

Did you implement something you learned from the previous chapter? If so, briefly describe the experience:

If not, please reconsider doing it this week.

Emotional Fibromyalgia (EF) is the petri dish or cultivating environment that collaborates with our Inner Critic to distort and exaggerate our perceptions of reality. While our Inner Critic belittles and challenges our ability to exert the effort required to achieve significant goals, EF exaggerates the height of the psychological mountains we must climb to achieve them. It distorts our view from the base of those mountains, making them appear more daunting than they actually are.

Researchers at the Mayo Clinic describe the condition called Fibromyalgia as one "that amplifies painful sensations by affecting the way your brain and spinal cord processes pain signals..."[iii] For most people, a gentle pat on the shoulder is a friendly, supportive gesture. Someone with Fibromyalgia may experience that same gentle attempt at reassurance as excruciating pain.

Similar to Fibromyalgia, people with EF experience greatly exaggerated levels of emotional discomfort as a result of their lack of healthy emotional benchmarks. Like the Inner Critic, EF is established and nurtured within the context of parent-child interactions. It's a prominent feature in overindulgent families, and our increasingly permissive, excuse-filled modern society.

When someone with EF experiences emotional discomfort, they may also experience a complete sense of overwhelm. As a result, they resort to tension-relieving activities at the expense of their goals. Regardless of the distraction of choice—food, drugs/alcohol, pornography, binge-watching television, etc.—excessive engagement in one or more of them reduces our resolve to overcome obstacles. These distractions provide temporary relief from emotional discomfort and divert our attention from life challenges and the effort required to address them.

EF helps fuel our Inner Critic and make its job easier. It exists across a spectrum that ranges from Mild EF to Extreme EF. Together, Inner Critics and EF lull us into complacency with various pleasurable distractions. They form a potent one-two punch to keep us mired in mediocrity.

No goals are formulated within a vacuum. Understanding our internal

Psychological Mountains

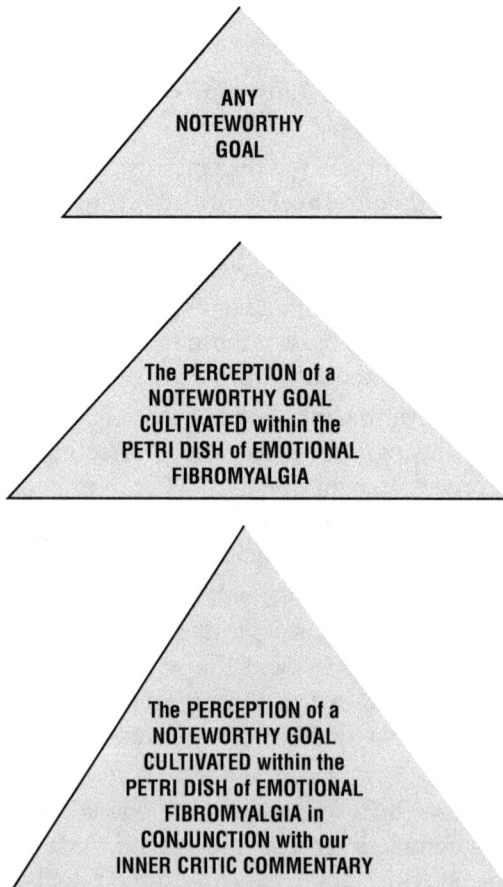

ANY
NOTEWORTHY
GOAL

The PERCEPTION of a
NOTEWORTHY GOAL
CULTIVATED within the
PETRI DISH of EMOTIONAL
FIBROMYALGIA

The PERCEPTION of a
NOTEWORTHY GOAL
CULTIVATED within the
PETRI DISH of EMOTIONAL
FIBROMYALGIA in
CONJUNCTION with our
INNER CRITIC COMMENTARY

and external constraints (EF and Inner Critic commentary) from the outset and developing productive countermeasures increases our ability to approach our goals with optimism and achieve them with considerably less effort.

The following example illustrates the impact of thoughts/perceptions on our emotions and our behavior. It also describes the origin and expansion of EF and how protective, but especially overly protective, parent-child interactions contribute to the condition.

How We Perceive Discomfort

Imagine that five individuals have been tested to determine their objective tolerance to physical pain. The medical exams conclude they all experience pain in the exact same way. Coincidentally, all five of them broke their right pinkie finger. The first individual refused to seek medical attention. He believed his level of discomfort didn't warrant the time or expense of a doctor visit. The remaining four rushed to an Urgent Care for treatment.

They're examined by different physicians who set their fingers and then ask them to rate their level of pain on a scale of one to ten (1Low–10 High). Based on their responses, the medical professionals decide on the appropriate pain medication. Since all four have the same level of pain tolerance, you'd expect them to rate it with the same numerical value. Patient #1 rates her pain at seven. Objectively speaking, this is an accurate assessment. Interestingly though, the other three rate their pain respectively as two, ten, and ten. So, what accounts for those differences?

Patient #2 rated her pain as a two. While driving away from the clinic, she complained to her husband that her finger was "killing her." When he vents his frustration and asks, "If you're in that much pain, why did you rate it as two?" She replied, "I didn't want the doctor to think I'm a baby."

Patient #3 rated his pain at ten. He later admitted he was drug-seeking and hoped the doctor would overprescribe pain killers. Patient #4 also rated her pain as ten but for a very different reason. Throughout her entire life, she had been raised in an overly protective environment. First her parents, and then others, treated her like a "princess." Rarely, if ever, had she been "allowed" to experience even the slightest degree of physical or emotional distress.

On the rare occasions when she did experience discomfort, her parents, nannies, teachers, boyfriends, and others immediately swooped in to remove it. (Consider the 1835 Hans Christian Anderson tale, The Princess and the Pea, as a point of reference). The doting and overprotective environment that was intended to protect her proved to be "too much of a good thing" and ultimately had a damaging effect.

Those experiences left her without objective benchmarks for discerning varying levels of discomfort. Without them, she evolved into a "drama queen" or "snowflake." Regardless of how minor her discomfort, she came to believe that it was beyond her ability to tolerate. The more she was "protected" from reasonable life challenges, the more her innate EF evolved into Extreme Emotional Fibromyalgia (EEF). Having been swaddled in metaphorical bubble wrap severely stunted her ability to deal with the physical and emotional realities of adulthood. It also strengthened her Inner Critic commentary by exaggerating routine events into psychological mountains.

She, like many others, believe that their world comes to an end when their cell phone dies, their game console breaks, or their boss asks them to come to work an hour early. Typical responses to such routine experiences may include:

"Why do these things ALWAYS happen to me?!"

"When will I ever catch a break?"

"Why does my boss hate me?"

Sometimes they trot out Murphy's Law, "If something can go wrong, it will." Their enablers continue to give tacit approval by nodding in silent assent or joining in on their defeatist mantras.

Other Manifestations of EF

In my private practice, I encounter individuals with Moderate EF (MEF) to Extreme EF (EEF) on a regular basis. Rarely do they tell me they're sad, though many do say they're "depressed." Clinical depression is a real medical condition, but when people confuse sadness with depression, their hyperbolic language promotes a more dramatic response.

They routinely exaggerate their level of discomfort by telling themselves (and anyone who will listen) that the word "sad" fails to accurately describe the extent of their subjective experience. According to them, their sadness is unbearable, and therefore they must be "depressed." Once they convince themselves they're depressed, pharmaceutical companies are only too happy to reinforce their misperceptions and sell them medication, whether it's clinically indicated or not. If their doctor is unwilling to prescribe the desired medicine, they'll doctor shop until they find one who will.

EF occurs on a spectrum ranging from mild to extreme. While physical and emotional discomfort serve as a protective measure to alert us that something's amiss, EF artificially lowers a person's tolerance so that everyday concerns are elevated to crisis level. Their overreactions are an external reflection of their internal, hyperbolic turmoil. While an extreme emotional response to a bear attack is reasonable, reacting the same way to losing a TV remote is inappropriate and reflective of EEF.

Choose your Words Carefully

The words we use to define situations limit our options for more appropriate alternatives. Hyperbolic language intensifies emotions and results in more extreme behavioral responses. It fans the flames of EF and distorts our perception of objective reality.

Overreacting is a manifestation of our internal hyperbolic conversations. When someone justifies their overreaction to a routine situation, it's a reflection of the often unconscious conversations they had with themselves beforehand.

For example, a young, former client named Angelo was caught shoplifting candy from a local supermarket. When asked about it, he was adamant: "I was starving man! I was freakin' starving!"

While he may have been hungry, I was quite certain he wasn't "freakin' starving." His over-the-top internal chatter elevated his mild discomfort of wanting a candy bar to overwhelming hunger that justified stealing. Rather than engage in a ridiculous verbal tug-of-war, I acknowledged his distorted perception and offered an alternative view.

"So," I asked, "You were starving, huh?"

"Yeah man. I was freakin' starving."

"Well," I said, "the KitKat* bar you stole was full of empty calories. So, the next time you're freakin' starving, I suggest you steal something more nutritious like a stalk of broccoli." The look on his face told me he got my point. He seemed to understand that I knew BS when I heard it. Although I never followed up with the supermarket manager, I'm quite confident there was no spike in broccoli theft in the weeks that followed.

Those who experience EEF desperately seek to expel their discomfort, so they can return to a state of emotional equilibrium. Like Angelo, they overreact to minor discomfort as if it's a calamity. They also demonize anyone they believe is responsible for, or who prevents them from relieving, their discomfort. The bottom line in this instance is don't stand between Angelo and a KitKat bar.

Parents who wittingly or unwittingly conspire with their children to avoid the discomfort of personal responsibility and defend a child's aberrant behaviors promote the development of EEF. When children act out and are pacified rather than held accountable, they're encouraged to

* KitKat is a registered trademark of The Hershey Company

repeat and even escalate their inappropriate behaviors. Through their distorted perceptual lens, they justify dysfunctional overreactions that become their habitual patterns. Adults who allow themselves to be held hostage to a child's unreasonable demands promote behavioral patterns in the child that reinforce EEF and are increasingly difficult to alter.

Although our family tries to avoid fanning the flames of our grandson, Mikey's, natural EF, the impact of some of these influences are inevitable and periodically seep into his psyche. When our daughter-in-law Keria told him, "You have homework this weekend." He placed both hands on his head and replied, "If I have to do homework, it'll be a catastrophe!" Clearly this is a manufactured catastrophe. It's neither urgent nor important. While it does reflect the experience of a young child who's inclined to embrace EF, it also reflects a youngster with a great vocabulary.

Individuals with mild to moderate EF are distracted by their discomfort, but they can usually manage it while attending to more important concerns. It's like walking down the street with a pebble in their shoe. Sure, it's uncomfortable, but it's tolerable. They remove it when they have a chance to sit down. Those with EEF experience that same pebble in their shoe as if they're running a marathon on a bed of hot spikes. They become so focused on the real or imagined intensity of their discomfort that they lose sight of the impact their response has on others. In extreme cases, parents who are so driven by their desire for relief from their own physical/emotional distress neglect or even abuse their own children.

Summary

EF navigates a parallel path with Inner Critics and thrives in environments where caretakers routinely remove the physical and emotional hurdles that promote healthy development in children. This results in children, and later adults, who are unwilling to even attempt realistic challenges. Their Inner Critic further exaggerates this perception with messages like:

It's too much effort. You know you can never do that. It's futile. Why bother trying?

The roots of EF grow even deeper when parents fervently defend children in the face of legitimate concerns from teachers, coaches, and even law enforcement officials. It's incredibly damaging. Whenever our comfort zone contracts, we become less inclined to exert the effort to address new challenges. This hastens a downward spiral into self-indulgence.

Exercise #10: *Document Your Discomfort Baseline (EF)*

Before deciding on a destination, it helps to know your starting point. Some people begin a weight-loss regimen by documenting their eating habits. Many are surprised at how much they underestimated their daily caloric intake. You can use a similar journaling approach for documenting your thoughts and emotional responses to various life events over the course of the next few weeks.

Completing this exercise will help you determine your EF baseline and save you time in the long run. Your Inner Critic will want you to skip or rush through these exercises, but don't fall into that trap. The exercises are step-by-step opportunities to get out from under its thumb. Documenting your patterned responses and ability to withstand discomfort will provide insights and suggest more productive paths forward.

Complete Exercise #10 in your workbook.

Exercise #11: *Give Meaning to Your Discomfort*

Emotional discomfort, particularly around goal achievement, is often an indicator of our Inner Critic's efforts to fan the flames of EF. Uncomfortable feelings are preceded by demeaning messages that alert us to the rapid approach of the boundaries of our comfort zone. Our Inner Critic wants to stop us in our tracks and maintain the status quo. It's threatened by anything with the potential to alter its dominance.

The late, great actress Katherine Hepburn admittedly experienced a high level of anxiety just prior to appearing on stage. On several occasions, she retreated to her dressing room and proceeded to throw up. Rather than viewing her discomfort as an excuse to retreat from the challenge, Ms. Hepburn powered through it. Once she was through throwing up, she'd wipe her chin and say something like, "Well, I'm glad that's out of the way. The show must go on."

Practice tolerating and even embracing mild physical discomfort and mild to moderate emotional discomforts. Ask yourself questions like, "Is my discomfort the temporary price I pay to achieve a goal, or will continuing down this same path cause even greater harm to myself or others? What would happen if I powered through my discomfort rather than use it as an excuse to quit?"

Consider this small step I took to expand the boundary of my comfort zone. When I counseled children at a local elementary school, I was annoyed by the crooked pictures on the walls between classrooms. My internal, mildly hyperbolic language exaggerated my discomfort, and I felt compelled to straighten them. A few days into the start of the new year, I made the conscious decision to ignore the imperfections and live with my discomfort. Eventually, they didn't bother me anymore, and I expanded the boundaries of my comfort zone.

Remind yourself that discomfort is an inevitable component of successful effort. A diabetic with low blood sugar may exhibit symptoms of fatigue, headaches, or lightheadedness. Their body is telling them to eat carb-rich food. Their discomfort can be a life-threatening event and should be addressed. However, the physical discomfort that accompanies a new workout regimen or the effort required to achieve an important goal is usually a sign that we're on the right track and should take it in stride. Some anxiety is to be expected when considering a career change, committing to marriage, or applying to graduate school, but it should not be the deciding factor in our decisions.

When we refer to the typical swirl of uncomfortable emotions and their physical counterparts as "bad," our instinctive reaction is to eliminate them. Not surprisingly, we may turn to old standbys like cigarettes, alcohol, Netflix*, a quart of ice cream, or whatever relieves our immediate discomfort. The problem with these solutions is that they delay or preclude more productive responses. The more we give in to them, the more our Inner Critic will manufacture additional excuses for putting off more important activities. On the other hand, productive action that focuses on solutions tends to reduce our anxiety.

It's important to recognize and work through the emotional rigors that are a natural part of life. Wallowing only gets us bogged down and stuck in the pain. When avoiding and removing discomfort altogether is our habitual response, unresolved issues remain unresolved, and we remain stuck in a downward spiral of our own creation. Here are a few steps to help you become more comfortable with tolerating and embracing discomfort.

Step #1: Notice when and where any signs of physical discomfort appear in your body.

Step #2: Identify the thoughts that accompany those feelings.

---

* Netflix is a registered trademark of Netflix, Inc

Step #3: Progressively tense and relax your muscles, without straining yourself, and hold your breath for a count of five. Then exhale and relax.

Step #4: Close your eyes and consciously escalate this event by intensifying the anxiety-producing thoughts a little bit at a time. Stop when you think you're approaching the boundaries of your tolerance. Quickly take more deep breaths and relax. Caution: Practice only MILDLY upsetting events such as your dog tracking mud across your clean floor.
Increase your anxiety a little each time you practice. This will increase your tolerance in a safe space.

Step #5: Now ask yourself, "Was that as bad as I imagined it would be?" Then answer that question. Your response may go something like this, "I thought I was either gonna die or at least explode. Yet neither of those things happened. It's uncomfortable, but I can handle my feelings better than I thought I could. This is the beginning of a new chapter in my life."

Practice this exercise daily for a week and then once a week thereafter. Notice the differences in how you experience stressful situations. Allowing yourself to experience and tolerate increased levels of discomfort is an important exercise for expanding your comfort zone, thereby reducing your EF.

We can boost our immunity by inoculating ourselves against the steady progression of EF to more extreme forms of the condition—Moderate Emotional Fibromyalgia (MEF) and Extreme Emotional Fibromyalgia (EEF). A strong, emotional immune system slows the growth of EF and allows us to deflect the allure of other Inner Critic influences. Embracing minor discomforts builds our emotional muscle, so we can resist them. It's like a baseball player taking batting practice. The more they practice, the easier it is to recognize incoming pitches, adjust their swing, and improve their batting average. Strengthening our emotional muscles allows us to deflect or redirect more of our Inner Critic commentary.

Running away from our emotions is conceding conscious control of our lives. When we embrace our discomfort by decoupling the thoughts that we've linked to those feelings, we reclaim our power. The realization that we can survive challenging emotions and even thrive is liberating. Your Inner Critic works tirelessly to keep you mired in a hopeless, victim mind-set. It'll use every devilish trick at its disposal to construct your comfort zone on wet cement. Then, it'll to divert your attention with pleasurable distractions until the cement dries and your feet are permanently affixed to the floor.

Identify one thing you'll implement this week based on Chapter 4:

CHAPTER FIVE

HOW SOCIETY NURTURES EF AND OUR INNER CRITIC

Did you implement something you learned from the previous chapter? If so, briefly describe the experience:

If not, please reconsider doing it this week.

To paraphrase a quote first attributed to Saint Bernard of Clairvaux (1091–1153): the road to hell is paved with good intentions. Unfortunately, fully capable adults allow themselves to be victimized by their Type I Inner Critic's intentions to protect them from any discomfort. Many aspects of modern society promote and reinforce our innate sense of entitlement, a perceived "need" for immediate gratification, and a dependence on external sources in place of personal responsibility. Others use their Type II Inner Critic's lies as an excuse for failing to accomplish their goals.

The truth is: people are usually helpless or victims to the extent they believe they are. Despite strong objective evidence to the contrary, many people remain unconvinced of their own power to challenge their subjective internal dogma. The media, corporations, public institutions, academia, and government all play roles in reinforcing our EF and dependence on them or other external forces.

Constantly lowering our threshold for discomfort makes it easier for Inner Critics to entice us with pleasurable alternatives. This keeps us focused on our discomfort rather than the rewards of achievement.

C'mon man. You know how hard that is. It's not worth it. You never take time for yourself. Relax and enjoy the little time you have. You don't live forever!

The gradual shift from occasional guilty pleasure to addictive, time-consuming pastimes is nearly imperceptible. Many people spend inordinate amounts of time and energy engaged in their favored mindless distractions. This can be another trap of our own design. They simply keep their head down and follow the trail of delectable crumbs that keeps them engaged. Many never awaken to the reality of their largely wasted potential.

Like all habits, when our patterned response to discomfort is avoidance, it's increasingly difficult to revert our effort toward more productive pursuits. Technological advances also predispose us to develop more extreme forms of EF. The more accustomed we are to the conveniences of modern life, the more difficult it is to do without them. Avoiding the discomfort associated with goal achievement lowers our tolerance in general as well as our tolerance of others.

Many years ago, power windows in vehicles and TV remote controls were viewed as luxuries until the cost came down and made them more affordable to the masses. In time, we grew accustomed to these conveniences. Many people get visibly annoyed when they're forced to hand crank their windows or get up from the couch to change the TV. Just ask my grandson, Mikey. He knows a lot about catastrophes. Changing the channel without a remote control or hand cranking a car window are things no civilized human being should ever have to do, right?

It's more than a linguistic mistake to refer to minor inconveniences as anything other than just that—minor inconveniences. Hyperbolic language heightens our upsetting thoughts and intensifies our anxiety. It drives many people to seek refuge from their discomfort in seemingly harmless diversions. Unfortunately, those harmless diversions often evolve into full-blown addictions. If you think that's an overstatement, try taking an iPad away from a teenager or a cell phone from an adult.

The remainder of this chapter presents various societal influences that deliberately or unwittingly amplify our EF. Each of them illustrates the impact slick, and often insidious, influences have on our lives. You'll see their collective impact and understand how they support our Inner Critic goals, lay waste to our potential, and keep us mired in a life of mediocrity (as we define it).

Netflix or "Crack TV"

Consider the similarities between crack cocaine and Netflix. Netflix, or "Crack TV,"

concentrates television shows down to their essence. It's like distilling hundreds of pounds of coca leaves to manufacture a single pound of cocaine. With the push of a button, we can access thousands of commercial free TV shows and movies. Like cocaine, Netflix is the purest form of TV bliss and has a similarly intoxicating effect.

Like other parents of adult children, we often rely on ours to help us with various electronic devices. So, it came as no surprise when our oldest son, Michael Ben, volunteered to help me set up our Netflix account when we first moved to Denver. We always get a chuckle when I share our experience. He began by explaining the basics, "See Dad, when one show ends, another one cues up within 20 seconds. I'll show you when this episode is over."

Just as predicted, when the credits rolled on the screen, a banner appeared on the screen informing us that the next episode was cued up and ready to go. Then, Mike's impatience got the better of him. "Screw this," he said. "I'm not waiting 20 seconds."

He pushed the button to start the next show right away. This incident presented a stark contrast to my experience as a youngster. Of course, that was a long, bygone era that only lives in the "fairy tales" I tell my grandson. Back then, we weren't able to record shows and had to suffer through commercials. When I missed an episode, I had to wait for summer reruns to see it.

In seventh grade, one of my favorite TV shows was the campy Batman and Robin series starring Adam West. Each weekly episode ended with a cliffhanger where Batman and Robin were caught in some trap, like dangling over a vat of boiling lava. The dastardly Joker, Riddler, or Penguin would leave them struggling to escape while we were forced to wait a whole week to find out what happened. How could the Dynamic Duo possibly escape such a predicament? Somehow, the Caped Crusaders and I managed to survive a whole week, waiting for the less-than-dramatic conclusion that always fell short of expectations. Every Thursday night, I rushed to our living room and waited with bated breath—"same bat time, same bat station." These types of experiences taught me that I could weather the storm of uncomfortable emotions.

Mike went on to explain another Netflix feature. "When a series is over dad, they recommend other shows they think you'll like." Essentially, Netflix is saying, "If you like Crack TV, we also recommend Meth TV, Heroin TV, and Alcohol TV."

Moderate Netflix viewing, like any other distraction, can be a relaxing way to spend an occasional evening, or on rare occasions, the better part of a weekend. It only becomes a problem when binge-watching becomes a way of life. Many people live vicarious lives watching their favorite actors achieve their career goals while they dream of being discovered by a famous Hollywood director from the comfort of their basement.

Few individuals would ever consciously decide to allocate hundreds, or even thousands, of hours of their limited time on earth watching every episode of a TV series multiple times. Sadly, that's exactly what many people do. I have firsthand knowledge of several lost souls who watch TV for hours without moving a muscle. They're glued to their easy chair, consuming fast food and beer that's delivered to their door. Then they fall asleep. When they wake up, they wipe the pizza crumbs off their face and replay the portions of the shows they missed. Their lives mirror the directions they used to put on shampoo bottles: lather, rinse, repeat. Wake up, restart Netflix, call for food and alcohol delivery, eat and drink themselves into a stupor and then go back to sleep—ahhhhhhh, the American Dream.

Challenging our Inner Critic is hard enough without having to deal with others who align themselves with its goals. Enticing external influences collaborate with our Inner Critic and strive to keep us permanently adrift in the tranquilizing fog of mediocrity. This makes it increasingly difficult to manage routine emotional challenges. The remainder of this chapter focuses on a wide range of societal influences that reinforce EF and attempt to keep us "hooked" on various mindless pursuits and easy, though irresponsible, ways to avoid emotional discomfort.

Substance Use

Legal Painkillers

The United States comprises a mere 4.4% of the global population. Yet, estimates from various sources indicate that Americans consume 30%–80% of the world's legal painkillers. Until recently, TV marketing campaigns led us to believe that the total eradication of pain through narcotics was a better choice than the alternatives. They either failed to mention the potential downsides or quickly rushed through the disclaimers using jargon that only lawyers understood. They also featured actors engaging in upbeat activities as they enjoyed carefree lifestyles. The subliminal suggestions were that narcotics would make you pain free, happy, and energetic.

Advertisers understand and exploit our tendency to surrender to EF. The American populace is already primed to avoid minor discomfort. Those experiencing excruciating pain are further compromised. They're more likely to give in to these "irresistible" marketing campaigns that promise relief. Another commercial portrayed young, active adults with opioid-induced constipation. But there was no need to panic. Pharmaceutical manufacturers marketed another medication to address that condition. This never-ending process shapes consumer appetites. It leads us to believe we must be 100% pain free and perfectly comfortable all the time. Repeatedly the message is, "Why suffer when you don't have to?" and "Total pain relief is achievable." They'd have us believe we're stupid if we choose to suffer "needlessly."

Although there are legitimate medical reasons for consuming marijuana and it's not a narcotic, it is a mind-altering substance. Since its legalization in the state of Colorado, the city of Denver now boasts more marijuana dispensaries than McDonald's and Starbucks combined. The "natural" progression of temporary, recreational distractions can lead to addictive habits that also promote an increase in our EF. Embracing distractions lowers our tolerance for discomfort. A lowered tolerance for emotional discomfort feeds our Inner Critic's narrative that we're incapable of addressing life challenges and must remain in close proximity to our emotional medicine cabinet. Of course, the sale of these addicting substances keeps the pharmaceutical companies happy and their cash spigots flowing.

Illegal Drugs

The U.S. is the largest market for illegal drugs. Approximately 80% of the global opioid supply is consumed in the United States.[iv] This is like a Trojan Horse for our foreign adversaries. It destroys the fabric of our society from within and forces us to reallocate resources that would otherwise be utilized to strengthen our national defenses, rebuild aging infrastructure, etc. Illegal drugs negatively affect the lives of individuals and their families and shatter human potential.

Alcohol

Here are a few sobering statistics on alcohol abuse. They reflect the challenges many people face tolerating, managing, and expressing their feelings in socially appropriate ways. They provide another example of a temporary cure for EF.

An estimated 88,000 people (approximately 62,000 men and 26,000 women) die from alcohol-related causes annually. Alcohol is the third leading preventable cause of death in the United States. The two larger problems are tobacco abuse and a poor diet.[v]

All three causes of death are a reflection of EF and our struggles with emotional regulation. About one in four college students report academic consequences from drinking, including missing class, falling behind in class, doing poorly on exams or papers, and receiving lower grades overall.[vi]

The consequences of underage drinking[vii] include increased risks for:
- School problems, including higher rates of absenteeism and poor or failing grades.
- Social problems, such as physical aggression and lagging participation in youth activities.
- Legal problems, such as sexual or physical assaults.
- Unwanted, unplanned, and unprotected sexual activity.
- Higher risk for suicide and homicide.
- Changes in brain development with possible lifelong effects.
- Accidental death from alcohol poisoning.

In addition, the personal and financial costs to families, lost worker productivity, and treating alcohol abuse are incalculable. Despite the commonly stated phrase, "I need a drink," it's exceedingly rare that anyone actually dies of a lack of alcohol. So, do I really "need" a drink? Or have I convinced myself that common emotional challenges require self-medication for comfort and survival?

Performance-Enhancing Drugs

Many athletes are willing to risk their careers, their physical and emotional well-being, and even their lives by taking performance-enhancing drugs. They willingly place their health in jeopardy for the lure of enhancing athletic performance. In fact, a whole industry is dedicated to helping athletes bypass legitimate testing protocols.

Physicians, companies, coaches, and even governments supply "clean" urine specimens, masking agents, or my personal favorite, the Whizzinator.* As of October 2020, the Whizzinator website describes the product as a "... discreet synthetic urine kit that is safe for all types of scenarios. It has the most life-like realistic fake penis on the market... Our synthetic urine formula is so realistic, it has foam and scent!"

Apparently, there isn't anything illegal with selling a Whizzinator — it's only illegal to use it for its intended purpose.

What would happen if athletes competed on a level playing field, and everyone accepted the results of their untainted efforts? Unfortunately, far too many athletes, trainers, sports teams, and gamblers view the short-term rewards associated with winning at any cost too tempting to resist. Despite the risks, it's easier and too financially rewarding to cheat. This reflects the

---

* Whizzinator is a registered trademark of Alternative Lifestyles Systems, Inc.

lengths to which some people will go to protect themselves from the discomfort associated with personal responsibility and supports the transition from EF to EEF.

Academia

Grade Inflation

Here are two useful definitions for grade inflation: "(1) grading leniency: the awarding of higher grades than students deserve, which yields a higher average grade given to students (2) the tendency to award progressively higher academic grades for work that would have received lower grades in the past."[viii]

In many schools, grade inflation is commonplace. Many teachers and school administrators have firsthand experience dealing with pressure from students, parents, and coaches to give some students better grades. Even in graduate school, students may be offered extra credit opportunities to improve grades in areas that are only loosely related to the course material. In my case, I worked very hard and received an A grade in a graduate statistics class. That was NOT the grade I earned nor is it the one I should have been given. I was given an A because I completed a bunch of unrelated extra credit assignments.

Hard work does not always warrant a higher, or even passing, grade. When teachers inflate grades, there are fewer objective standards to distinguish students. The short-term benefits of unearned grades feel good in the moment to students and teachers. However, there are less obvious, long-term consequences for graduates and the employers who want to evaluate them.

Exerting consistent effort to study is hard and causes discomfort. Many people consider discomfort bad. Pressuring teachers to inflate grades is one way to relieve that discomfort. Some students go so far as to demonize anyone who challenges their "right" to better grades.

Test Anxiety

As a former student services coordinator and adjunct instructor, I worked with a large number of students who regularly failed exams. They claimed that test anxiety was the culprit. Of course, it's normal to experience some level of anxiety even when we're adequately prepared. However, the vast majority of students who sought special accommodations from me for the unseen, catch-all phrase "test anxiety" were quite open about the fact that they hadn't bothered to study.

I was a strong advocate for special needs students and took my responsibilities very seriously. I was determined to level the playing field for those who struggled with learning difficulties or physical challenges. Often there were simple strategies that would help them meet their academic goals.

However, most of the students seeking accommodations for test anxiety did not have a legitimate claim. Some claimed it was unfair that others were "naturally gifted" and didn't have to study. They thought it was my job to tilt the playing field in their favor and provide accommodations that would eliminate their need to study altogether. Most of them were unreceptive to my recommendation that they study — and study hard. Instead, their responses ran the gamut from whining, talking smack behind my back, taking it up with a department chair, cheating, or even dropping out of school altogether. Some even blamed me for their inertia and making their lives miserable.

It's understandable that students initially try to resist the rigors of studying if they think there are less strenuous alternatives. However, when their excuses are rejected and they're forced to choose between studying or failing (or cheating), most will grudgingly study. I don't blame them for trying though. Everyone has some innate degree of EF and naturally seeks the path of least resistance. Students who use any excuse as "their excuse" continually expand their EF and provide additional fodder for their Inner Critic. They claim fictitious academic challenges, throw up their hands, and quit. Students with EEF are convinced they're unable to withstand the emotional rigors of studying. Exerting consistent effort over time is hard and uncomfortable. Their logic? Discomfort is bad. Anyone who causes them discomfort is mean. They believe they're justified in relieving that discomfort in whatever way they deem appropriate.

Is this starting to sound familiar?

Diploma Mills

Why earn a legitimate degree when you can bypass the college experience altogether?

Simply pay for a diploma without completing the work. Diploma mills are phony universities that sell college degrees and transcripts without a legitimate academic experience. They're scams that hand out fake diplomas to anyone who pays the "tuition." They are usually much less costly than attending a legitimate institution. Hundreds of diploma mills exist throughout the U.S. and abroad. Completing legitimate academic work is hard and causes discomfort. People with EEF feel that employers are "mean" or "unfair" when they expect someone to earn a legitimate diploma; it's easier to falsify academic credentials.

Their EF provides them with a muscle memory excuse to sidestep personal responsibility. It reinforces their narrative that the emotional price is too high. Meanwhile, their Inner Critic runs alongside to remind them that they're incapable of success anyway.

You're too incompetent, unworthy, or lazy, so why bother? Lots of people have phony degrees or cheat their way through college. Otherwise, they couldn't stay in business.

Finances, Electronics, and Accolades

Credit Card Payoffs

Note: I realize that some credit card companies engage in deceptive practices, and some people experience financial hardships for legitimate reasons. Those are NOT the individuals I'm discussing in this section. The individuals I refer to here are those who recklessly overspend well beyond their means and then expect a bailout.

TV and radio advertisements encourage consumers to seek forgiveness for their credit card debt. The announcer boldly asks, "Are you deep in credit card debt?" "If you owe more than $5,000 in credit card debt, don't let the credit card companies 'TRICK YOU' into thinking you owe the whole amount."

According to the logic of these advertisements, we can rack up a ton of credit card debt and then wriggle out of our previously agreed upon repayment schedule. Seriously!? What leads anyone to think we can call the debt forgiveness company, or our metaphorical mommy or daddy, to bail us out when we make irresponsible purchases beyond our ability to pay?

We all claim to be adults, but some people make exceptions for themselves when it comes to handling their financial responsibilities. They feel that somehow the system is rigged and stacked against them. Debt forgiveness seems like a great deal, except for the rest of us who are forced to cover the cost of those who live beyond their means. Whatever the source of their discomfort, overspending provides a temporary respite. Rather than face the consequences of their irresponsible behavior, some even go on a spending binge and ring up new charges in anticipation of a bailout from a debt forgiveness company. Is this any different than the alcoholic who gets smashed the day before their scheduled entry into rehab?

Trophies for Everyone

To paraphrase the comedian Cristopher Titus, "When did everyone start getting trophies for sucking? If this happened when I was a kid, my mantle would be filled with trophies. This one's for when I sucked at football, that one's for me sucking at baseball, soccer, and so on." Somehow, many in our society have come to believe that kids should never be exposed to setbacks because they lacked the talent to be champions. How do we prepare children for the challenges of life when we insulate them from the possibility of defeat? Doing so only serves to enhance their EF and stirs their Inner Critic from its slumber. It reinforces the childish notion that they should only play the game if they're assured a trophy.

Time-Saving Devices

If we believe the TV commercials and print advertising, there are a myriad of time-saving devices designed for the sake of our convenience. Many people are convinced that minor, even ridiculous inconveniences require an "as advertised on TV" intervention. One commercial promotes an effortless way to remove the shells from hard boiled eggs.

It begins with an obviously frustrated woman who's forced to peel eggs the tedious, sweat-filled, old-fashioned way. Peeling eggs used to require as much as 30 seconds of valuable time that could be spent doing other things. Thanks to this "revolutionary" egg-shelling device, we can spend even more time watching Netflix. While watching this commercial with a friend, I innocently asked her, "Who's in such a rush for hard boiled eggs?" To which she replied (I'm not kidding), "What if I was expecting friends over and forgot to make the deviled eggs?"

"Oh of course," I replied, "I forgot about those egg emergencies."

Thousands of years ago, Socrates said, "Necessity is the mother of invention." A more relevant restatement for our time is that "inconvenience is the mother of invention." Nowadays, someone invents a product and convinces gullible consumers with EF that they can't live without it. An electric egg sheller is just one of countless examples. To quote Thomas Tusser, "A fool and his money are soon parted."

The following statistics reflect other social influences that play into our innate EF and, over time, contribute to Moderate or Extreme forms of the condition.

- The obesity rate in the U.S. topped 40%.[ix]
- 2.6% of the U.S. population has some type of gambling issue. That adds up to nearly 10 million people in the United States who struggle with gambling.[x]

- 8.5% of Americans between the ages of 8 and 18 (that's roughly 3 million people) are addicted to video games.[xi] (This data was published April 21, 2009; those statistics have surely risen since that time.)
- 50% of teens say they "feel addicted" to their mobile devices.[xii]
- 59% of parents think their teens are addicted to their mobile devices.[xiii]

Summary

Americans enjoy unprecedented amounts of leisure time. EF enablers rush to fill the void with various, tension-relieving activities and devices. The cumulative effect of this all-pervasive messaging to avoid or relieve all discomfort is undeniable. Removing every speck of effort makes the challenge of achieving mature adulthood even more difficult. It teaches us to be less resilient and more dependent on others. Routinely giving in to these societal influences makes it increasingly difficult to escape our natural tendency to expand the boundaries of our comfort zone.

Prelude to Chapter 5 Exercises

When we attempt a new challenge, flabby emotional muscle makes the determined effort even more daunting. By embracing the discomfort associated with the tying our own shoes (before the advent of Velcro), peeling our own eggs, earning decent grades, paying for luxuries we can afford, etc., we thwart the steady progression toward more EF and its cunning partner in crime, our Inner Critic.

Have your guilty pleasures blossomed into addictions? How much time do you engage in tension-relieving rather than goal-achieving activities? Managing emotional discomfort is an essential aspect of goal achievement, which is why it's important to embrace routine discomfort rather than shy away from it. Surrendering to EF only begets more extreme forms of EF. Conscious awareness and a moderate degree of self-restraint will help you resist your natural inclination to surrender to the "creeping disease" of EF. The exercises that follow will help with this process.

The Market Research Group Nielsen estimates that American adults spend more than 11 hours per day watching, reading, listening to, or simply interacting with (electronic) media.[xiv] A conservative estimate of spending as little as 3 hours per day on mindless electronic pursuits is equal to 21 hours per week or 1095 hours per year. That's the equivalent of more than 27, 40-hour work weeks per year. What constructive goals could we pursue if we reallocated a few of those 27 work weeks per year?

When video game consoles first became available to consumers, my wife bought me one for Christmas. For several weeks, I'd rise early to play for an hour before work. One leisurely Sunday I got up to play, and the next thing I knew, it was dark outside, and twelve hours had passed. I packed the game console up and never played it again.

We can all use a little break from time to time. However, I quickly realized that my "well-deserved" breaks grew to consume much of my life and made significant priorities an afterthought. How many gamers consciously plan to average three or more hours per day for 10 years (or more) playing video games? That's the equivalent of gaming 3,650 hours, or 24 hours per day for more than 152 days. I have better things to do with my time.

You may be surprised at how much time you spend on inane timewasters beyond their restorative benefit. If you're not convinced, try giving up your favorite electronic device for a week. If you experience symptoms of psychological withdrawal such as increased tiredness, insomnia, anxiety, irritability, etc., you're probably spending more time on them than you realized. The more we give into the tug of EF, the more irresistible it becomes. Inner Critics celebrate every increase in EF because it strengthens their grip on power. The point of Exercise #12 is to identify how many hours you engage in pleasurable distractions beyond what's reasonable for you to refresh and re-energize your spirit. Then consider how much time you'd like to reallocate for more productive pursuits.

Complete Exercise #12 in your workbook.

Exercise #13: *A Simple Riddle*

Reflect on this riddle before rushing to my answer below. "What do the following individuals have in common?" Jesus Christ, Mahatma Ghandi, Abraham Lincoln, Joan of Arc, Martin Luther King, Jr., John F. Kennedy, Robert Kennedy.

Take a minute to reflect on your answer before reading my answer below.

Answer to Exercise #13 Riddle

Agree or disagree with their philosophies or goals, they're all considered great leaders. In addition, they all died for their beliefs. When we discover our life purpose and clarify our guiding values, our passion to achieve them will naturally follow. We'll know when we've succeeded in defining our life purpose when we too are willing to die for our beliefs. I have no doubt that these individuals had a vocal Inner Critic and were tempted by their own pleasurable distractions. However, their Inner Critic chatter was minimized or isolated when they focused on their life purpose and guiding values. We can do likewise.

Identify Your Higher Purpose

At about the age of seven, I was channel surfing between the four available channels on my old black and white TV. Like I said, it was a long time ago. While switching stations, I happened upon a rather forgettable movie with a single memorable scene. An elderly farmer on his deathbed was surrounded by loved ones when he shared his final thoughts. He told them his biggest regret was that he failed to accomplish certain goals, not because he tried and failed, but because he was too afraid to try. He pleaded with them to learn from his mistakes and sidestep the petty fears that could prevent them from chasing their dreams.

Even at the tender age of seven, that powerful message resonated with me. Although my death seemed a million years away, I knew I didn't want to leave this life with regrets like that sad, old farmer. In time, the movie gradually faded from my consciousness. However, it reemerged when I was in my mid-twenties while browsing through a bookstore. It was then that I ran across a poster that read, "There are three types of people. Those who make things happen, those who watch things happen, and those who wonder what happened."

It rekindled the memory of the promise I'd made to myself. I made plans to identify my life purpose, my values, and my goals, and I began to take concrete action to move toward their achievement. I refused to squander anymore time watching my life go by wondering what happened.

Many people stumble through life, wandering in aimless circles with one oar in the water. They latch onto one pleasurable, inconsequential pursuit after another, or they allow others to define their success. Like the old farmer, many never snap out of their lifelong hypnotic trance before they run out of time. They sell their soul for momentary pleasures rather than true purpose and contentment.

Some measure success by the number of toys and vacations they accumulate, the size of their bank accounts, or other momentarily satisfying "shiny objects." There's little doubt that these things can make life more enjoyable. However, ultimate success and contentment is not dependent on external items or circumstances. The comedian Jim Carey said, "I think everybody should get rich and famous and do everything they ever dreamed of, so they can see that it's not the answer."

Earl Nightingale defined success as, ". . . the progressive realization of a worthy goal or ideal." If someone is working toward a predetermined goal and knows where they're going, that person is a success. Success is not a single remarkable achievement, no matter how grand. It's always a moving target. Realize a goal, celebrate it, but avoid resting on your laurels before moving onto the next one. Many of us are reminded of our life priorities in the midst of a crisis. Consider how you might handle the following scenario.

Imagine that you're babysitting a four-year old family member. Normally, he's well behaved, but on this occasion, he's unusually fussy and demanding. On top of that, you've come down with a migraine and an unsettling stomach bug. Despite feeling under the weather, you realize you need a few items for dinner. You strap the youngster into his safety seat and head off to the supermarket. Once inside the store, the child continues his tantrum. You can almost read the minds of other shoppers, "Can't you make that brat shut up?"

You resort to bribery and finally a few mild whacks on the backside. All to no avail. Thoroughly frustrated, you scoop the child into your arms, rush through the checkout line, and drive home. As you sit down to dinner, you sternly inform him, "It's supper and then off to bed for you, young man."

After tucking him in, you make a beeline for the bathroom where you proceed to puke up your guts. Some say there's no such thing as a stupid question. I disagree. This multiple choice question will challenge that assumption. With your head still hanging over the toilet, you hear an intruder breaking into your home with the intention of hurting the child. Would you:

    a. Direct the intruder to the child's room because you were upset with his behavior in the supermarket?

    b. Politely request that the intruder come back in an hour when you're feeling better?

    c. Do whatever you can to protect the child?

Obviously, the situation is urgent. In those emotionally charged moments you'd find the inner strength to rise above your petty feelings of frustration and physical illness. Without giving it a second thought, you'd instinctively do whatever you could to protect the child. Regardless of the intensity of our life challenges, they're mere flickers in relation to the bright light of our clearly defined purpose.

Why wait for an unlikely emergency? Keeping our life purpose and values as our internal backdrop diminishes the power of our Inner Critic and helps us sidestep our EF. It propels us along our chosen path with the focused energy of a laser, like when we're defending the life of a child. It makes us less prone to overreacting to challenging circumstances. When an emergency arises, we can panic, choose the first available path, and hope to get lucky. Or we can prepare by keeping our life purpose at the forefront. In the words of the Roman philosopher Seneca, "Luck is what happens when preparation meets opportunity."

Planning our life on purpose helps us determine our goals and set a path to achieving them. It prepares us for unexpected emergencies and enables us to act instinctively with directed urgency and calm assurance. One way to do this is by writing your eulogy. This allows you to begin at the end of your life and work your way back to the present moment. You can delineate a life without regrets and place both oars in the water as you travel upstream. It's a powerful tool that's often more challenging than you might imagine. Keep at it.

Your Inner Critic may work overtime to convince you that these exercises are too hard or too time consuming. It'll try to distract you with your favorite "shiny objects." However, sidestepping the dismissive messages and maintaining your focus will weaken its efforts to dissuade you. It'll illuminate your path with a purpose, diminish your Inner Critic's authority, and reduce the urge to give in to your EF.

On September 9, 2011, United Airlines Flight 93 was hijacked by four al-Qaeda terrorists. The plane was averted from crashing into the U.S. Capitol when a heroic group of passengers and crew members overpowered the terrorists and forced a crash landing into a vacant field in Pennsylvania. The life purpose and highest values of those heroes came into sharp focus in the face of that unexpected crisis. Few people are prepared for such an event. When your moment arrives, will you be a hero or a lamb led to slaughter?

Exercise #14: *Write Your Eulogy and Epitaph*

Feel free to use the Sample Eulogy Format as a guide.

Sample Eulogy Format

Imagine your home is consumed in flames, and you have moments to flee with your life.

1. Write down the few items you'd take with you.
2. Record the highlights of your life to date as short bullet points.
3. Describe your remaining life goals and why achieving them are so important to you.
4. Explain how achieving these goals impacted your life, the lives of your loved ones, and/or society as a whole?
5. Decide how you want to be remembered by the most important people in your life. Provide a few examples that stand out as humorous or reflect your unique contributions. Think about how you acted or will act when your "crisis" happens.
6. Reflect on your life with gratitude and mentally or literally thank those who've impacted you or served as inspiration. Some may be pleasantly surprised to learn how you feel about them.

Once you complete your eulogy, condense it into a few words or sentences to serve as your epitaph. This will provide you with a personal mantra or mission statement. It will help you maintain your focus, regardless of external circumstances. Crafting your eulogy allows you to determine your life direction and leave a legacy (however you define it).

Identify one thing you'll implement this week based on Chapter 5:

_____

_____

_____

_____

SECTION FOUR

KNOW YOUR ADVERSARIES AND CULTIVATE ALLIES

CHAPTER SIX

UNDERSTAND YOUR
INNER CRITIC'S TACTICS

Did you implement something you learned from the previous chapter?
If so, briefly describe the experience:

_____

_____

_____

_____

If not, please reconsider doing it this week.

For the better part of my life, I've engaged in impassioned battles with my Inner Critic; the ultimate control of my thoughts, emotions, and behavior was at stake. Although I've finally gained the upper hand, my Inner Critic remains my most challenging adversary. Our current interactions can be summed up in this adaptation of a quote from the Dalai Lama: if you think your Inner Critic is too small to make a difference, try sleeping with a mosquito.

I unmasked my Inner Critic for the first time that long-ago Saturday morning. When I did, I had no idea whether it was possible to alter our relationship. In the midst of my uncertainty, there was an uncomfortable gnawing in my gut and a deep sense of discontent in the dark recesses of my mind. Somehow, I knew I was capable of much more than what I'd accomplished to that point in my life. Still, I wondered, "Is it possible to overcome my Inner Nemesis? Could I detangle myself from its web of lies and forge a new path forward? If so, how the hell do I begin?"

My response to those questions began when I took a fresh look at my relationship with my father.

Giving Up the Ghost of My Past: My Type I: Benevolent Protector—Internal Dictator

The imprint of my relationship with my father continues long after I left the family nest more than 40 years ago, and he remains a steady presence long after his passing. Rather than view my life as a series of separate, unrelated events, I began to examine the tapestry of our lives and saw just how much they were interwoven. It revealed recurring patterns and how his childhood experiences shaped his worldview and became a blueprint for our relationship.

Both of my parents grew up during the Depression Era. Mom described her upbringing as generally uneventful. She was the youngest of eight and grew up in a loving and intact home. In contrast, a somewhat turbulent childhood had a significant impact on my dad. His father (my paternal grandfather) died at the relatively young age of 45, a few short months after dad's 13th birthday. His mother had issues of her own, and parenting wasn't exactly her strong suit. In addition to the emotional and financial strains he faced as a result of his father's early death, dad also battled a chronic heart condition after a bout with rheumatic fever.

In those days, the world was a very different place. Emerging from the Great Depression, the United States and her allies collectively beat back the threat of Nazi Germany and Imperial Japan. In the aftermath of those major events, America confronted a new threat—world communism. The Cold War heightened indirect hostilities between the U.S. and former Soviet Union, while the Korean "hot" conflict exacerbated global tensions. With a collective fear of the "Red Menace," Americans lived under the constant threat of nuclear annihilation. Many families spent a small fortune on personal bomb shelters. The threat was not some abstract theory. It was a very real possibility! Like dad, most of the citizenry were caught up in a frenzy of fear, paranoia, and patriotic fervor. New hostilities could've flared up in any number of foreign hotspots.

Lacking the counterbalancing influence of a consistent father figure and resentful of his mother's overprotective tendencies, dad was determined to prove his manliness. At the age of seventeen (1947) and against the wishes of his mother, he convinced his grandfather to sign enlistment papers, and he joined the Marine Corps. In the days that followed, the country remained in a permanent state of heightened readiness. I can only imagine the intense emotional strain this placed on a generation of young adults.

Dad took his oath to protect our country very seriously, and he applied that same level of dedication to raising us kids. He "perfected" his parenting style in the Marine Corps and was determined to fend off the debilitating impact of indulgent parents like my grandmother. He considered it his solemn duty to prepare us for the many threats we'd inevitably encounter through-out our lives. He also replicated some of the same tactics that helped transform a generation of raw recruits into battle-hardened marines. We were like fresh arrivals at Paris Island (Marine Boot Camp), and he was our drill sergeant. His stern admonitions became a template for my Inner

Critic's script. While my Inner Critic continues to include harsh rhetoric in his arsenal, dad eventually understood his missteps and mellowed considerably in his later years.

Despite his immense intelligence and keen insights, dad also had his share of blind spots. He greatly overestimated our ability as children to discern the difference between intentions and messages. We were just immature kids with a limited ability to navigate the turbulent waters of our formative years. He viewed us as miniature versions of himself and acted accordingly. His name-calling and sarcasm belied his fundamentally loving intentions. He wanted us to push past our fears and overcome the obstacles that stood between us and our goals.

Initially, it worked. When I succeeded at something, it was usually more out of fear of disappointing him than confidence in my own abilities. I mistakenly internalized the outwardly demeaning commentary that drowned out his good intentions. Unfortunately, it was those the harsh messages rather than his loving intentions that became his unintentional legacy. As an adult, I now understand, and I consciously choose to reject his messages and embrace his intentions. Dad's parenting style was neither good nor bad, right nor wrong. It was, however, one of his Misapplied Strengths. He reflexively borrowed from successful leadership experiences in the Marine Corp and erroneously applied them to parenting. As misguided as they were, he clearly acted out of love. He was convinced, and often with good reason, that he knew better than us kids—his "raw recruits."

Interestingly, my older brother, John, had a very different take on dad's ear-splitting critiques. He entered adolescence during the counterculture years of the mid-1960s. His reflexive tendency was to disagree with dad's more traditional perspectives. This often placed them on a collision course. On the other hand, I usually shared dad's conservative views. At times, my outward compliance allowed me to minimize or sidestep his wrath. We still had our share of intense run-ins, but as I recall, they were less frequent than those between dad and John. John was the firstborn. It's likely that this further contributed to even greater scrutiny. He solely bore the burden of dad's high expectations for nearly four years before I entered the scene.

In his senior year, John was accepted to a small college in Louisville, Kentucky. It was a 13-hour drive from our home in Philadelphia. It came as a complete shock that he would even consider a school that far away. After all, how could he possibly succeed outside the protective confines of our home environment? In my mind, our parents made sense of our world. John was excited by new possibilities; I was terrified. John sought physical and emotional distance from our family. Where he saw freedom and opportunity, I saw fear and failure. When I took my first tentative steps toward independence, it was like peering through a pipe that was pointed directly at the sun. Everything in my sky was obscured by the bright light of dad's all-encompassing presence. John, on the other hand, viewed life through a wide-angle telescope. In many ways, our lives were similar, but the lens through which we viewed life made a huge difference in our perspectives. (See the illustration below). Although John never lost sight of our father's presence, dad was just one among many celestial objects in his field of vision.

**My View of Life
Through a Pipe**

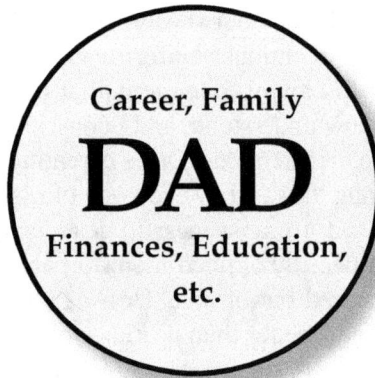

Career, Family

DAD

Finances, Education,
etc.

**John's View of Life
Through Wide-Angle
Lens Telescope**

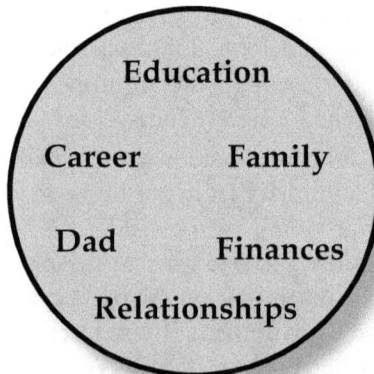

Education

Career   Family

Dad   Finances

Relationships

Tactic #1: Perceptual Narrowing[3]

Perceptual Narrowing was my Inner Critic's first weapon of choice. It skewed my view of the universe and severely limited my options. It prevented me from seeing anything other than what my Inner Critic wanted me to see. My view allowed me to be lazy. It provided a convenient and consistent structure with easy-to-follow instructions. All of my options existed within the confines of my comfort zone. Whenever I was exposed to novel ideas that contradicted my Inner Critic's messaging, he'd tip my telescopic pipe back to the same, predictable paths of complacency and assured mediocrity. It rarely occurred to me that alternative views existed outside that framework.

I routinely brushed aside encouragement to try something new. However, the more that reliable sources challenged my Inner Critic's undisputed assumptions, the more I began to question his messages. Perhaps I wasn't as inept and unworthy as I had come to believe. If what people were telling me was true, then I might have been mistaken all these years. The more others reassured me of my competence, the more I began to cautiously consider that possibility.

My introspective journey began when I asked myself a few, tentative questions. Of course, it was naïve of me to expect objective and forthright answers. Since my Inner Critic continued to frame and dominate my internal conversations, his responses were understandably dismissive and unsatisfactory. After all, my Inner Critic's sole purpose was to keep me stuck.

It was as if I flashed back to second grade at St. Andrew's Catholic School. The nun, who'll remain nameless, gave similar answers to my seemingly innocent questions. I still remember sitting at a desk in my starched white shirt and emblematic dark blue tie. I'd raise my hand and ask questions like, "Sister? If God is all good, why do we have to die?" "Well, Mr. McCafferty. That's called a mystery. You'll find out if you go to heaven."

In other words, "I don't know. Just believe what I say without question. Besides, you're annoying me. Keep it up, mister, and I'll have to call your (Marine Corps Sergeant) father. We wouldn't want to do that, now would we?" "No sister!"

I'd then avert my gaze to my desktop where my fingers were reverently intertwined. A deep sense of shame would come over me for daring to question anything. She was sending a signal to me and all the other students: "Don't ask questions or else there'll be trouble. Just shut up and obey!"

---

[3] Perceptual Narrowing is the tendency to restrict our focus to a single idea to the exclusion of others. The singular thought is particularly prevalent at times of heightened emotional arousal.

Similarly, when I posed questions to my Inner Critic like, "If I'm so stupid and unworthy, why do so many credible people tell me otherwise?"

Of course, he didn't have any good answers. He just expected me to fall in line as if I was still that dumb second grader at St. Andrew's.

Obey without question, or I'll get really upset. Do I have to yell at you to remind you who's the boss?

It was the beginning of more epic encounters. For my Inner Critic it was like fishing with dynamite. Whenever questions rose to the surface of my mental pond, he'd toss in a stick of dynamite and blow them up. Like my nun, he never felt the need to provide a credible answer.

Shut up and obey! Don't question me!

My response might as well have been, "Yes sister," and that would be the end of it. Now, conscious awareness of my Inner Critic's existence allows me to place mental deflectors in place and implement effective countermeasures. Although I'm more seasoned and confident in my abilities, I also understand that I can never count my Inner Critic out entirely. He always reappears to varying degrees whenever I confront new challenges or consider new goals. The difference now is that I see nearly limitless possibilities beyond my original telescopic vision.

I've learned better than to simply roll over and submit. Even so, I still have days when I'm tempted to pull the covers over my head and join the old farmer from the black and white movie of my youth. I may even climb into an adjacent deathbed for a spell. However, I've realized that battling my Inner Critic is an ongoing, lifelong process; those feelings will come and go. I know I'll get over them, and this inspires me to persist despite the challenges. I no longer allow my Inner Critic or previous setbacks to permanently define me.

Tactic #2: Attacking My Competence with Disparaging Remarks

Tactic #2 was by far my Inner Critic's most direct and straightforward maneuver. His approach with Tactic #1 was more subtle and usually below my conscious awareness. When Tactic #1 failed, my Inner Critic switched to Tactic #2: Attacking My Competence with Disparaging Remarks. By the time he resorted to this tactic, he was frustrated and confused with my defiance and noncompliance. Tactic #2 was easy to identify because he was so confrontational. The veins on his forehead throbbed as he angrily grabbed his megaphone to crank up the volume. He screamed insults and reminded me of my countless real or imagined shortcomings. He'd generate more excuses for inaction—some dripping with sharp and unforgiving sarcasm.

YOUR'E SOOOOO RIDICULOUS! . . . YOU'RE NOT SMART ENOUGH! . . . YOU'RE TOO OLD! . . . IT'S TOO HARD! . . . DON'T WASTE YOUR TIME! . . . WHERE'D YOU EVER GET THE STUPID IDEA THAT YOU COULD ACTUALLY DO THAT?!!!

Our Inner Critic presents itself to varying degrees whenever we consider a new goal or confront a new challenge. I also maintain a heightened awareness of the physical signs that alert me to his presence. My neck and shoulder muscles tense, my thoughts begin to race, and I get an uncomfortable feeling in the pit of my stomach. These are all signs that my Inner Critic has entered the room.

Although his messages are often harsh, his intentions are ALWAYS designed to protect me from ALL forms of discomfort. He never distinguishes between the degrees of discomfort or the potential benefits of working past the various forms of it. It's up to me to decide whether to shy away from it (as in the case of an approaching bear) or to embrace the possibility of a rewarding experience (as in the case of a promotion).

Once he accepts the futility of this Tactic #2 approach: Attacking My Competence with Disparaging Remarks and grows weary of berating me, he resorts to Tactic #3.

Tactic #3: Increase EF and Distract with Shiny Objects

Tactic #3 is just another arrow in his quiver. It includes two steps — Increasing Emotional Discomfort and Distracting with Shiny Objects. For years, my Inner Critic used Tactic #3 to get the upper hand. The process went like this:

Step #1: Increase Emotional Discomfort

The constant drumbeat of self-limiting and disparaging messages caused my emotional discomfort to spike.

C'mon Mike. Do you realize how hard that is? You've never been good at _____. Your chances of failing are astronomical. It's a fool's errand to even try. Persistence has never been your strong suit.

My Inner Critic would use this type of messaging to convince me that whatever the challenge, it was impossible for me to overcome. When I stewed over these thoughts, I felt defeated and often gave up without a fight. This was his way of luring me away from working through the emotional discomfort associated with a challenge.

Step #2: Distract with Shiny Objects

Once my anxiety reached a fevered pitch, he'd dangle my favorite tension-relieving activities or "shiny objects." My favorite "shiny objects" include food and endless hours of TV. Overwhelming feelings are nothing that three or four cupcakes and several hours of TV won't cure—at least temporarily. Those and other mind-numbing "guilty pleasures" quickly degenerated into major time wasters. The more I engaged in them, the more addictive they became, and my intolerance for emotional discomfort soared. This made those pleasurable distractions all the more irresistible.

C'mon Mike. Another game's on TV. . . . Just one pizza and then you can get to work. . . . Everyone's going out for a drink. You only have to have one . . . you already had one drink. All your friends are drinking . . . you might as well have another.

When my sugar high wore off, I got sleepy and went to bed. This tactic was very effective. First, my Inner Critic employed hyperbolic language to exaggerate my level of discomfort. Then, he minimized the consequences of engaging in pleasurable distractions. With food, TV, and so many other diversions within easy reach, it became increasingly difficult to consistently pursue productive activities.

We all know that stressful life events are inevitable. Sometimes my Inner Critic would even convince me to take preemptive steps to inoculate myself before they occurred. I was like an alcoholic who drank a beer to "take the edge off" just in case something might happen.

Ya never know Mike. It's better to be safe than sorry. One cupcake (that turned into three or four) won't hurt.

After eating four cupcakes, I was in no condition to exercise. Instead, I'd take a nap, wake up with a headache from the excess sugar intake, and then allow my Inner Critic to control the narrative once again.

You're a weak and pitiful slob. You'll never get in shape. Since it's never gonna happen anyway, just accept it and have another cupcake.

Complacency became a way of life, and the walls surrounding my comfort zone continued to expand. I excluded more and more mildly challenging activities. The path of least resistance became my only viable option. Newton's First Law of Motion states, "A body at rest stays at rest (unless another force acts upon it), and a body in motion stays in motion." In my case, my ass on the couch tended to stay on the couch.

It took me a while before I realized that Tactic #3 was just another trick. It began as a temporary respite but evolved into a way of life. Once I realized the trap, I began the slow climb out of my sugar-coated coffin, set new goals, and made some headway toward their achievement.

Premature Victory

"Free at last! Free at last! Thank God almighty we are free at last!"

—Martin Luther King Jr.

... or so I thought. I assumed that Tactic #3 was my Inner Critic's final act, and I allowed myself to be lulled into a false sense of security. Since he could no longer control me with his previous tactics, he shifted gears and temporarily slipped out of sight. While I was busy celebrating previous victories, he quietly plotted his next moves from an underground lair. In the meantime, I got cocky and let my guard down. What I had interpreted as ultimate victory was merely an illusion. The balance of power only appeared to shift in my favor. It took a while to figure out that flattery was the next step in our psychological arms race. And so began his deceptive, guerilla campaign.

Tactic #4: Flattery

The predictable prelude to Tactic #4: Flattery, began with a quick run-through of the previous Tactics #2 and #3. It's easy to recognize now, in retrospect. He'd begin by raising the volume on my internal loudspeaker and blare the loudest and most disparaging comments he could muster. When I steadfastly refused to bend to his will, he'd elevate my emotional discomfort and dangle more pleasurable diversions. After I successfully defended myself from those frontal assaults and sat down to celebrate those hard-won victories, my Inner Critic would waive the white flag of surrender and give me a head fake. It was then that he seamlessly transitioned to Tactic #4: Flattery. I thought the war was over. However, he replaced his verbal assaults with rose petals. He appealed to my vanity. To paraphrase Sherlock Holmes, a new game was afoot.

C'mon Mike. You just finished a long week at work. What more do you have to prove? When are you going to take a well-deserved break? You already have a comfortable lifestyle. There's no need to be greedy. You've already done enough. You expect waaaaay too much of yourself. I get tired just thinking of your effort. You deserve some time to relax. Have another soda to wash down your cupcakes. Besides, you are now getting sleepy.

His attempts to "befriend me" caught me off guard. It was my Inner Critic's most cunning modification. It took me months to realize what was behind the revised commentary. He purposely used the softer, gentler approach to dupe me yet again. If possible, he'd have literally fluffed my pillows, massaged my shoulders, and handed me another cupcake. The dramatic shift was so confusing that it stopped me dead in my tracks. It stunned me into apathy.

Of course, that was exactly what my Inner Critic had in mind. His faux adulation convinced me to settle in for a nice, long break from challenging myself. The more I savored the attention, the more I remained stagnant or lost ground toward important goals. New opportunities slipped by before I realized it. My complacency erected new and even taller psychological mountains to climb. I reverted to unhealthy eating habits and stopped exercising altogether. In short order, I regained the 40 pounds that I'd lost after two years of consistent effort. The more weight I gained, the harder it was to exert the discipline and energy required to lose it. Once again, lethargy was my constant companion. After regaining the upper hand, my Inner Critic reverted to form.

He'd beat me up for letting myself get out of shape. Then he'd increase my emotional discomfort and ply me with delectable enticements. It wasn't long before my life reverted to trivial pursuits. All the while, my Inner Critic rested comfortably in a nearby tree with the self-congratulatory grin of a Cheshire Cat.

After several months with my ass stuck to the couch, I realized it was my Inner Critic who was serving up the flattery. That's when I decided to get back to work. I gave up my secret stash of cupcakes. I returned my focus to career and family. Tactic #4: Flattery was my Inner Critic's most Machiavellian[4] effort to date.

Summary

I have no doubt that the original inspiration for my Inner Critic was my father. Knowing the original source of your Inner Critic is far less important than recognizing its existence, its purpose, and its tactical progression. Conscious awareness allows us to devise effective countermeasures. The sequential tactics of my Inner Critic included perceptual narrowing, increasing EF and distracting with shiny objects, attacking my competence with disparaging comments, and its most insidious tactic—flattery. Over time, I began to appreciate the fact that Inner Critics are flexible and use any tactic that serve their purpose: to protect us from emotional discomfort. Heeding their efforts resigns us to a life of mediocrity and falling short of our full potential.

---

[4] Someone who is Machiavellian is sneaky, cunning, and lacking a moral code. The word comes from the Italian philosopher Niccolò Machiavelli, who wrote the political treatise The Prince in the 1500s, that encourages "the end justifies the means" behavior, especially among politicians.

Exercise #15: *Determine Your Highest Values*

The path to achieving a truly satisfying life occurs when our highest values align with our life purpose, and we follow that path. The more we focus on them, the more our EF, inertia, and Inner Critics become distant flickers. However, remaining true to our highest values seems easy until two or more conflict with each other.

Several years ago, I was forced to choose between protecting our daughter, Hannah aka Sugar Bear, and respecting her privacy. She had just graduated from high school and had experienced some emotional challenges. It was out of character for her to mope around the house for more than a day, and she was reluctant to discuss whatever was chewing at her. My wife and I were understandably concerned, but we also wanted to respect Sugar Bear's space. In my effort to understand and provide emotional support, I decided to read her diary.

Gasp! Yes. I read the diary of an 18-year-old woman without her knowledge or consent — and I'd do it again! (Sugar Bear gave me permission to share this anecdote and the brief comments taken from her diary.) I didn't rifle through the entire diary beginning with page one. Instead, I opened it to the last page and worked my way forward one page at a time until I uncovered what was so upsetting. It turns out that she was sad about her (lame) former boyfriend dumping her.

She went on to write that despite her sadness, she knew she'd be okay. She expressed gratitude for her faith and her family and was confident she'd make it through those difficult times. I remained concerned but also relieved. She was safe and that's all I needed to know. I continued to monitor her behavior from a distance. Naysayers adamantly disagreed with my decision. They proclaimed it an egregious offense to "invade" another adult's privacy, but can you imagine the backlash that would have ensued if I, her father and a counselor, hadn't read her diary and instead discovered her lifeless body hanging from the ceiling? Those same naysayers would demonize me for being blind to circumstances that unfolded in plain sight. My overriding concern for her physical safety was more important than my respect for her privacy.

I didn't then, nor do I now, give a damn about the naysayer opinions! Living up to our values may cause unwanted collateral damage. However, others don't have to like, agree, or live with our decisions. We do. I did what I believed was best for my daughter and for me. A nice, though unnecessary, confirmation of my decision occurred about nine months later when I told Sugar Bear what I'd done. Her reply was, "I figured you did, Papa Bear. I know how much you love me."

Determine your values and NEVER allow others to talk you out of them. As Shakespeare said, "To thine own self be true." Clarifying our values allows us to set the boundaries within which we'll live a life of purpose. Living up to our highest values, even when they conflict with less important ones, is likely to cause an emotional tug-of-war (as referenced in Question #11 of the Analogy Questionnaire). There are times when there are no perfect answers, and we're forced to choose between two or more imperfect alternatives. Even if Hannah had been outraged at my decision, I'd have gladly paid that price to ensure her safety and well-being. I continue to rest easy with my decision.

It's unlikely our values will completely change over time. However, their relative importance may evolve as we move through various life stages. For example, young adults without children may rate parenting as a low priority. However, if they marry and decide to raise children of their own or enter a relationship with a single parent, they may alter their view dramatically.

The internal tension we experience when our values and actions are out of alignment is a reminder that we can never escape the reach of our authenticity. The emotional angst can be quite intense. That disconnect is likely to increase our EF, which entices us to find an easy way out and seek immediate relief instead of resolving the underlying issues. It also puts our Inner Critic on high alert to berate us for the lack of alignment.

Clarifying our values and aligning them with a higher purpose allows us to maintain our focus on our most important goals. It helps us sidestep the distractions that might otherwise divert our attention. If you struggle to complete Exercise #15, ask yourself this question, "What do other people do that really upsets me?"

If you're outraged when someone lies or steals, then honesty and integrity are likely contenders for your most important values. If you rate two or more values the same, consider breaking the tie by reflecting on hypothetical situations where you're forced to choose between them. Any value you rate less than 7, is unlikely to be that important to you. After you finish the exercise, evaluate how your values align with your actions. The greater the discrepancy between how well you talk the talk and walk the walk, the more likely you are to experience the internal tension associated with those discrepancies.

Recognizing and understanding your values is an important step in the process of defining your guiding principles, addressing your EF, and winning the war with your Inner Critic. Without decisive and consistent action, the countermeasures described in this book will remain abstract theories, as inaction relegates important goals to a distant horizon that always remains just beyond grasp. By consistently applying these countermeasures, you will whittle away at your Inner Critic's iron grip and liberate your pent-up potential. Speaking for myself, I learned that an old dog can still learn new tricks.

Complete Exercise #15 in your workbook.

Identify one thing you'll implement this week based on Chapter 6:

_____

_____

_____

_____

CHAPTER 7

PEACE THROUGH STRENGTH:
BREAKING THE CHAINS OF ENSLAVEMENT
ONCE AND FOR ALL

Did you implement something you learned from the previous chapter?
If so, briefly describe the experience.

If not, please reconsider doing it this week.

Bullying Bullies

Some experts advise us to envision our Inner Critic as a demon and immerse ourselves in the role of invincible superhero. They suggest engaging in a life and death struggle to mortally wound and destroy all vestiges of its existence. I faithfully practiced this approach several times a week for many months, with limited success. No matter how hard I tried, I was unable to completely vanquish my Inner Critic.

My encounters mirrored those chronicled in ancient Greek lore between the Hydra[5] (my Inner Critic) and Hercules (me). Every time I cut off his head, two new ones grew in their place. Predictably he'd mock my effort.

What makes YOU, of all people, think you can destroy me this time after so many failed attempts?

The derisive comments only added to my frustration, so I fought back even harder. Finally, after countless failed attempts, I grew weary of swinging my heavy sword with nothing more than a tired arm and additional Hydra heads to cut off. It was time to try something different.

> "If at first you don't succeed, try, try again. Then quit.
> No use being a damn fool about it."
>
> —*W.C. Fields*

---

[5] The Hydra was a mythical serpent-like monster with many heads. If you cut off one Hydra head, two more would grow back in its place.

Inner Critics are both cunning and immortal. Barring brain surgery, it's impossible to eliminate them entirely. We can, however, minimize their impact. We can place them under house arrest while we cultivate healthier internal and external environments. Remaining vigilant helps us repel Inner Critic advances before they can strengthen their grip on us.

Long-Term Solutions

As humans, we instinctively try to protect ourselves from threats of any kind. Instinctive responses include: fight, flee, or freeze/cower. I found that chopping off my Inner Critic's head in simulated battles proved as effective as beating up the neighborhood bully. Initially it stopped him in his tracks, but he always returned to exact his revenge. I now subscribe to the more enlightened approach promoted by Patrick Laplante: "It's only when a mosquito lands on your testicle that you realize that violence is never the answer."

Effective countermeasures allow us to rise up from the ashes of our previous victimizations. This new approach requires that we reject the outdated and distorted beliefs our Inner Critic expects us to accept. Addressing an imminent threat is urgent, but once it's passed, it's time to resolve the underlying issue(s). Rather than relying on remedial measures like eating cupcakes until we fall asleep, we can implement more permanent solutions.

Specific bullying events may have ended months, years, or even decades ago, but they continue to reverberate in the minds of those who choose to revictimize themselves. We remain coconspirators with our Inner Critics until we interrupt the repetitive internal messaging. Just as maintaining unhealthy eating habits keeps us unhealthy, constantly replaying demeaning messages on a continuous loop fortifies the bars of our own emotional prison. To paraphrase wise counsel from the English writer Aldous Huxley, when did we get the idea that rolling in the muck is the best way to get clean? Victims who continue to wallow in the muck of a bully's disparaging comments do so because they believe that "muck" to be true. Giving credence to the distorted messages from our Inner Critic only invites more of the same.

By recognizing that aggressive behaviors are reflections of our bully's insecurities or Misapplied Strengths, we can view our experiences through a more objective lens. In most situations, physical aggression is frowned upon and characterized as inappropriate, but it can be useful or even lauded at times, such as when it occurs on the battlefield, inside a boxing ring. It only becomes a Misapplied Strength when its's used to bully others. Viewing aggressive behaviors through this lens removes the sting of judgement and allows us to put down excessive emotional baggage. Don't we have enough emotional baggage without adding more?

A significant way to diminish the power of any bully, especially our Inner Critic, is to forgive them—ALL of them. Even more importantly, we must forgive ourselves for being fooled into believing our Inner Critic's lies and distortions in the first place. Forgiving everyone frees us from the futility of fighting past battles and reaffirms our sense of self-reliance. Different times call for different methods, and these are different times. Forgiving everyone eliminates our need to waste emotional energy on replaying bullying incidents; it allows us to focus on important priorities. Forgiveness is in our enlightened self-interest.

As with any other habit, forgiving others may be difficult at first, but with practice, it can be done. Just as heroic first responders train to overcome their initial instincts and run toward danger, we can also learn to embrace the initial discomfort of forgiveness, especially after holding onto it for so long. As the Dalai Lama and others have said, "Forgive everyone for everything." It doesn't matter what they said or did or what you consider "reasonable" justifications for holding onto your bitterness. Forgiveness is the path to liberation and can help end our Inner Critic's reign of terror.

Craft Incremental Milestones that Lead to Goal Achievement

"Shoot for the moon. Even if you miss, you'll land among the stars."
–Norman Vincent Peale

Borrowing from Edward Maunder's astronomical phrase, "Seek your own Goldilocks Zone." The Goldilocks Zone refers to the habitable zone around a star where the temperature is just right—not too hot and not too cold—for liquid water to exist on a planet. In the same way, you need to design goals that stretch but don't break you. Design goals that stretch but don't break you. Setting the bar too low leads to boredom. Boredom provides our Inner Critic additional opportunities to delay, distract, and ultimately talk us out of exerting effort to achieve our goals. Paradoxically, Inner Critics may also encourage us to seek perfection and stretch beyond our current capabilities. The perpetual pursuit of perfection is a suicide mission. It gets very tiring. It wears us down and encourages us to throw up our hands whenever we fall short of achieving impossible objectives. Setting goals outside the Goldilocks Zone is an open invitation for our Inner Critic to berate us for falling short. Life is challenging enough without making unforced errors that give it additional ammunition.

Celebrate Efforts and Progress

Celebrate efforts even when they fall short. Affirmations, visualizations, maintaining a healthy diet, regular exercise, etc. are all incremental successes on the road to achieving your goals. Build on them and focus on progress toward reasonable milestones. Setbacks are only permanent if you allow them to be permanent. View them as signs that it may be time to consider another approach or double down on current efforts. Significant goal achievement rarely occurs in a straight line.

Distinguish between Intuition (Allies) and Your Inner Critic (Adversary)

Intuition is defined as the ability to understand something immediately from instinctive feelings without the need for conscious reasoning. In contrast, our Inner Critic is a sub-personality that judges and demeans us. When attempting to differentiate between the two, consider the tone and intention of the voice or feelings that bubble up from within. In potentially dangerous situations like driving on the highway, our intuition may provide a stern, uncomfortable nudge that something's wrong. "LOOK OUT! Danger ahead!"

Our Inner Critic may also warn us that something's wrong. It may present itself either before or in the aftermath of an event. Its tone and words are harsh and demeaning. It feels more like a punch to the gut. "LOOK OUT STUPID! ARE YOU TRYING TO GET US KILLED?!" or "LOOK OUT STUPID! YOU ALMOST GOT US KILLED!"

Notice your words and your emotions. They're clues as to whether the presence is a valued guest (intuition) or an unwanted intruder (Inner Critic).

Summary

Inner Critics are immortal. Bullying them (and other bullies) into compliance may feel good in the moment, but it's an ineffective long-term strategy. Forgiveness is an important key to releasing pent-up resentment and is the path to liberation. Build incremental milestones within your Goldilocks Zone, celebrate effort and progress, and distinguish between your intuition and your Inner Critic.

Your Inner Critic won't take your efforts to change the status quo lying down. Challenging it will generate defensive responses. It will use every tool at its disposal to dissuade you from taking back the reins to your life. Remain vigilant to its tactics. Your Inner Critic's success depends on your compliance and submission.

Exercises: #16A OR #16B

Possible Exercise #16A: *Targeted Visualization for Type I Inner Critic: External Protector—Internal Dictator.* In these cases, **Reject the Message — Embrace the Intention**

Exercise #16A deals with a Type I Inner Critic: External Protector—Internal Dictator. In these cases, the goal is to Reject the Message and Embrace the Intention. Our Inner Critics want to protect us from discomfort—even when a reasonable level is to be expected. They arise when we have looming deadlines or are contemplating new goals. They'll bombard us with discouraging messages until we either surrender to the exaggerated and hyperbolic discomfort, or we work through it.

The following exercise is specifically designed as a prophylactic measure to effectively and preemptively address your Inner Critic on a permanent basis.

Review and modify the following script to fit your specific situation. If you like, record a version based on the type of Inner Critic you are addressing and replay it in a private, relaxed setting. Practice five to ten minutes a few times a week until you can replay it in your mind without the recording.

If you catch yourself making excuses like, "I don't have time for this," ask whether that's objectively true or if your Inner Critic is trying to talk you out of it.

Step 1: Close your eyes and relax. Envision yourself as a young child in a private setting and make yourself comfortable.

Step 2: When your External Protector approaches, invite them in and direct them to take a seat directly across from you.

Step 3: Recall an early experience where your External Protector (or an adult caretaker) protected you from a potentially dangerous or emotionally challenging event.

Step 4: Then imagine yourself transitioning from that young child into a fully grown, confident adult. Breathe deeply through your nose and completely exhale through your mouth. Notice a bright,golden glow surrounding you in a warm, supportive hug. Feel your self-confidence build and surge through every cell of your being.

Step 5: Tell your protector, "Thank you for loving me and keeping me safe when I was a young child. I appreciate those intentions, but now I'm a fully grown adult and no longer need your protection."

Then continue with your version of forgiveness. It may go something like, "I appreciate your concern. I also forgive both of us for assuming I understood the difference between your messages and your intentions. Now I'm an adult, and I can handle these situations on my own."

Step 6: Finally, tell your External Protector, "Thanks for stopping by _____." Escort them to the exit and close the door behind them.

Step 7: Take a few deep breaths and continue to revel in your power and self-confidence. Bask in the afterglow of these feelings of empowerment.

Step 8: Confidently stride to the exit and return to your daily life. Return to the room as often as you like and repeat the process. In the event that your External Protector tries to argue, respond with a calm but firm mantra like, "Thanks for stopping by _____. I'll take care of it on my own. Have a good day."

Possible Exercise #16B: *Targeted Visualization for Type II Inner Critics: External Bully—Internal Dictator.* In this case, **Reject the Message and Reject the Intention**

Despite the similarities, there are distinct differences between the visualizations in Exercise #16A and Exercise #16B. With a Type II External Bully—Internal Dictator, you'll want to Reject the Message & the Intention. External Bullies seek to intimidate others with demeaning messages that reflect their own insecurities. Their messages DO reflect their intentions. They feed off their ability to intimidate and convince us we're incapable of _____.

Step 1: Close your eyes and relax your muscles. Envision yourself as you were during a specific bullying incident. Enter a private space and make yourself comfortable. Allow yourself to experience a small approximation of the uncomfortable emotions you experienced at the time of the bullying event.

Step 2: Envision yourself transitioning into a fully grown, confident adult. Breathe deeply through your nose and exhale completely through your mouth. Imagine a bright, golden glow surrounding you in a warm, supportive hug. Feel your self-confidence surge through every cell of your being.

Step 3: When your External Bully approaches, greet them and direct them to a seat across from you.

Step 4: Imagine them sneering and asking something like, "What do you want?"

Step 5: You respond calmly and confidently, "I want to discuss how you bullied me when we were younger" (even if it was just the other day).

Step 6: If they try to interrupt or blame you, firmly assert control of the conversation. "I'm not that person or little boy/girl anymore. I'll no longer allow you to torment me! I'm a strong and confident adult."

Continue to feel your confidence course through your veins. "I know that you were acting out of your own insecurities. You wanted to feel better about yourself because you felt so weak and insecure. The mean things you did and the lies told me were designed to make you feel better at my expense. I reject all of your bullying messages and your intentions to cause me harm. I reject them all!"

Step 7: Envision the bully slowly shrinking until they're less than half their original height. You can sense their shame as they apologetically look at the floor.

Note: It doesn't matter whether you think the person who bullied you would ever apologize in real life. If they're unapologetic, it's another reflection of their emotional weakness. This is your safe space to see past their dysfunctional bravado, to achieve peace within yourself, and to acknowledge their pain and weakness.

Step 8: With a firm and assertive tone, you continue, "You'll never torment me ever again."

Step 9: Watch your bully continue to shrink as you repeat mantra statements like, "I am in control of my own life, and I'll never allow you to torment me ever again." Watch your bully continue to shrink until they're no more than an inch tall.

(Ready for the MOST challenging part?)

Step 10: Continue to feel your confidence grow as you begin to feel sympathy toward your FORMER oppressor. Then tell them, "I forgive you for taking your insecurities out on me. I know now that bullying me was your attempt to fill your emotional void and to feel better about yourself." I forgive you for trying to convince me that your lies were true. I know better NOW. I also forgive myself for carrying around my self-doubts because I believed the nasty things you said. From now on, I'll decide what's true about me, how I feel about myself, and what I can achieve with my life. Your lies and distortions will never sway my opinion again."

Step 11: Then, firmly but kindly tell them, "It's time for you to go and never come back. I wish you the best." Then give the sad, tiny, inconsequential version of them a pat on the head and escort them to the exit. Then, lock the door behind them.

Step 12: Take a few deep breaths and continue to revel in your power and self-confidence. Allow yourself to sit with these feelings for as long as you like.

Step 13: Confidently stride out of the room to take on the next challenge, fully assured in your ability to address it.

Return as often as you like and repeat the process. While still basking in the afterglow of the exercise, consider the following possibility: how would you handle an unexpected encounter with a former bully in real life? Assuming that your physical safety is not at risk, consider your options. You might pretend like you don't see them, whether they recognize you or not. That is certainly an option.

However, what would happen if you quietly take some deep breaths, recall the warm, reassuring glow, and tell yourself, "I'm a fully capable adult, and I can handle this"? Confidently stride up to them and look them in the eye. Then extend your hand to shake theirs and calmly reintroduce yourself. You're likely to catch them off guard. They may not remember you, or they may be embarrassed about your previous interactions. It doesn't matter. Simply greet them and possibly engage in a minute of small chitchat, then say good-bye. They may not remember you or the bullying encounters. Either way, presenting yourself as a fully confident adult is an important milestone. They may walk away, impressed with this new and improved version of you. More importantly—you'll impress yourself as you continue to reset important interpersonal boundaries. It's also a good way to disarm your Inner Critic whenever you encounter it.

Exercise #17:

Others, friends and foes alike, won't take your efforts to change the status quo lying down. Changing your behavior inevitably alters the dynamics of your relationships. Dealing with your Inner Critic is hard enough, but your allies will also resist your efforts to alter the status quo. After all, they're accustomed to the "old you" and have a vested interest in keeping things the way they were.

Some may bristle at your efforts and refer to you in unpleasant terms like "cocky" or "overbearing." They want your return to the "old you."

"What happened? You used to be so nice. Now you act like such a jerk."

Or, "You used to be so calm, but now you're always so angry!"

Or the icing on the cake, "I like the old you better."

In effect they're telling you, "It's okay to assert yourself with others, but please go back to being a doormat with me." Understand that by failing to establish healthy boundaries in the first place, you share some responsibility for the present state of your relationships. Whenever you allow others to overstep your boundaries, you teach them it's okay to do so.

If you want to change the dynamics of any relationship, recognize the symbiotic nature of the old ones. It's likely that those who treat you poorly have unwittingly formed an alliance with your Inner Critic, and they feed off one another. If someone continually undermines your efforts, perhaps it's time to reevaluate those relationships altogether. Why would anyone who truly cares about you want to keep you stuck in an unhealthy arrangement? Your goal is to achieve mutually beneficial arrangements. When a friend or partner brings home your favorite dessert just as you start your new diet, kindly but assertively remind them of your intention to maintain your new lifestyle and return "the gift" or discreetly pitch it.

As with your Inner Critic, it's better to maintain healthy boundaries than clean up the mess that occurs in the wake of unhealthy interactions. When your allies openly or subtly, encourage you to revert to old patterns, they're acting out of their muscle memory in ways that worked in the past. Making changes to previously unspoken rules is challenging for all parties. Who likes to change their worldview?

Remember, you've been a willing coconspirator all along. So, take these opportunities to forgive rather than chastise others. Consider this a transition to a better life. Forgive yourself and forgive them. It's the beginning of a new era!

Exercise #17: *Mental Rehearsal*

Read through this sample scenario as a guide before clicking on the link below to access the worksheet for Exercise #17.

Step #1: Recall a troubling conversation in specific detail where someone had you doubting yourself. How did your Inner Critic reinforce those self-doubts? For example, how did your Inner Critic respond when your boss (or anyone) made a snide comment like, "We should have known better than to let you handle this project."

Step #2: Identify any uncomfortable physical sensations. Slow your breathing and continue to take deep breaths. Relax your muscles.

Step #3: Identify your related emotions.

Step #4: Identify the demeaning messages your Inner Critic replayed in the days that followed like "I'm such a loser. What the hell's the matter with me? I better start looking for another job."

Step #5: Rewrite the script in the present tense. How would you respond in a more productive manner? For example, imagine your boss made a comment like, "You REALLY screwed this one up! I should have known better than trust you to handle it."

You might respond with something like, "I'm sorry things didn't work out this time, Mr. Johnson. I think we all learned a lot. I'll certainly be better prepared next time. What do you think I could have done differently?"

Accepting responsibility for your role is a far cry from agreeing that you're a screw-up. Maintaining our composure in the heat of the moment may be difficult when we're unprepared. However, developing agile responses that fit the moment is like any other skill. You get better with practice.

Replay the situation in your mind's eye and/or in front of a mirror. Be sure to practice maintaining a calm and confident posture, relaxed facial expressions, and good eye contact. Write the new script for the way you'll ideally handle similar situations in the future.

Step #6: Once you feel confident in your private sessions, you may consider role-playing with a friend. Write both scripts and direct your partner how to act. The more you practice, the easier it is to respond to similar situations in the moment.

Mental rehearsal and role-playing will help you reclaim your power and diminish the unproductive spiral of demeaning comments from your Inner Critic. The most important result of this reconditioning exercise is that it provides a blueprint for future interactions.

Another important benefit is that others will notice the difference in your demeanor. They'll be less likely to approach you in an aggressive manner in the future. The more you practice and improve, the less you'll need to utilize those skills. Carrying yourself like a potential victim sets you up to be victimized, whereas acting and reacting with confidence invites respect.

Step #7: Schedule a follow-up meeting with the person who inspired your new scenario. Practice your script using self-assured (rather than cocky) body language.

Your script might read something like, "May I have a few minutes of your time, Mr. Johnson?" When he agrees to meet, say something like, "I want to assure you that I learned a lot from our recent setback. I want you to know I'll always give you my best effort and be better prepared next time.

Thank you for bringing this matter to my attention. I recognize my missteps, but I'm not a screw-up as you asserted in that meeting. I'd appreciate it if you'd avoid name-calling in the future. That doesn't increase my motivation to do my best for you."

Pause briefly and allow him to backtrack and apologize, or let things hang in the air for a minute before ending the conversation. Calmly thank him for meeting and leave.

Complete Exercise #17 in your workbook.

Another Way to Avoid Overreacting:

There are times when the best alternative to handling a difficult situation is to punt. By punting, I mean holding your tongue in the moment so you can "live to fight another day." Rather than make a situation worse by over-reacting (shouting or cowering), simply hold off until you're more in control of your thoughts and emotions. Firmly but respectfully ask to conclude the conversation another time. Punting gives you an opportunity to collect yourself and retrieve a productive script from your mental file.

Productive outcomes of punting that conclude with a follow-up session, include:

1. increasing your self-confidence in responding to external naysayers,

2. increasing your capacity for discomfort and stretching the boundaries of your EF for mastering emotionally challenging situations,

3. potentially turning a critic (boss or others) into an ally, and

4. placing a cork in your Inner Critic's mouth while increasing your internal, self-reinforcing Affirming Tower as indicated in Table 1.

When you overreact in the moment, you play into the hands of others and your Inner Critic. You send the message that you're unable to manage your emotions. It also tells them you can be provoked into overreacting. They're likely to store that information away and use it to their advantage in the future. They might even share this information with others to characterize you as an out-of-control nutjob. Your Inner Critic will also chime in to replay your overreactions and beat you over the head with them.

Exercise #18:

This final exercise is designed to avoid complacency. It allows you to monitor your relationship with your Inner Critic on an ongoing basis. It will normalize more productive responses to your Inner Critic and others. It's called The Inner Critic Encounter Sheet. You can use it to practice real-time responses during encounters with your Inner Critic and others or in the aftermath of such an encounter.

Complete Exercise #18 in your workbook.

Epilogue

When to Begin?

Right now! Procrastination is a trap. It's designed by your Inner Critic(s) to provide enticing alternatives to encourage you to give up before you get started or to quit when the going gets tough. Inner Critics will use the wasted time to sharpen their tactical knives to convince you to give up on yourself and remain stuck. Complacency is a creeping disease. Unless we remain vigilant, our Inner Critic will sneak up and reemerge with a vengeance. Our son, John, wrote a poem when he was just ten years old. It illustrates the importance of taking decisive action.

Magic Wand

I told my friend,
I found a magic wand.
He just laughed, so
I turned an ugly duck into a swan.

He still didn't believe me,
So, I turned a stick into a tree.
He said, "Yeah right."
So, I turned today into tonight.

Finally, he said,
"You're such a liar,"
Until I turned his hair to fire.
Now he believes me!

Will you make room in your life to achieve your most important goals, or will you wait for your hair to catch on fire?

"Choose wisely, grasshopper."
    —*Master Po*

The Cost of Your Investment in Your Future

Investing in yourself comes with a cost. But, as the mechanic in an old oil filter commercial so eloquently stated, "I told Joe a few months ago, he could invest $10 for an oil change. He didn't listen, so now he's paying $5,000 for a new engine. Like Joe, you can pay a little now or a lot later. Either way, you'll pay."

By investing a small amount now, you'll earn a large return on your investment. There are five basic reasons why you'd pass on these opportunities to invest in yourself by completing the exercises in this book. They are precisely what your Inner Critic wants. They include one or more of the following beliefs:

1. My situation is hopeless.

2. I have no control over my life circumstances, so why bother?

3. The exercises are stupid; why waste my time?

4. There are so many pleasurable distractions that are more important.

5. It's impossible to win the war with my Inner Critic—better to accept a life of mediocrity.

Where do you think those types of thoughts originate? Initially, challenging your Inner Critic may seem overwhelming and as inviting as diving into an icy pond. However, if you do decide to take the plunge, you'll quickly acclimate to the water and ask yourself, "Why was I so afraid?"

"Courage is what you earn when you've been through the tough times and you discover they aren't so tough after all."

—Malcom Gladwell

Completing these exercises will lower the self-imposed barriers that prevent you from achieving your most important goals. It'll increase your self-confidence, improve your ability to regulate your emotions, reduce your EF, and generate a triumphant sense of purpose. It will be the opening salvo to help you Win the War with Your Inner Critic.

Here are a few of my favorite quotes. I think you'll find them inspiring as well.

"Courage is doing what you're afraid to do.
There can be no courage unless you are scared."

—Eddie Rickenbacker, WWI Flying Ace

My personal favorite:

> "For all sad words of tongue and pen, the saddest are these: 'It might have been.'"
>
> —*John Greenleaf Whittier*

Recognizing the existence of your Inner Critic and its demeaning messages and tactics are important steps toward a more fulfilling life. However, without constructive action like the countermeasures identified in this book, you'll needlessly struggle with discontent, unfulfilled dreams and wasted potential. Take this opportunity to make the most of your life. You only get one. As General George Patton said, "A good plan—violently executed now—is better than a perfect plan executed next week."

Wishing you all the best on your lifelong journey to ***Win the War with Your Inner Critic.***

Manuscript Summary

The arrows correspond with the manuscript summary below. The direction of the arrows reflects the relative importance of each item in relation to sone another.

The purpose of this manuscript is essentially twofold. The primary focus is on winning the war with your Inner Critic, but there is an even broader purpose. Managing your Inner Critic in productive ways will be a catalyst to a more fulfilling lifestyle.

These tables illustrate the various elements of decision-making and their relation to one another. Each of them impacts our willingness and ability to address specific problems or work toward particular goals. I'll assume that number one is met and will focus on the remaining seven elements.

1. Your innate abilities.

   We all have certain innate abilities. However, one trait that's impossible to measure is the indomitable human spirit. We may not be a naturally gifted brain surgeon, but we may be able to become one if we dedicate ourselves to achieving that end and address the other items on this list. That said, it's important to accept certain realities and the laws of physics. I would love to play linebacker for the Minnesota Vikings, who could use some depth at that position. However, as a 65-year-old man who hasn't played organized football since the second grade, it's unlikely my desire and effort will be enough to compensate for my glaring shortcomings and the level of competition in the NFL.

2. The significance of the goal or challenge.

   a. The more important a goal is to you, the more likely you are to work on it.

3. Your ability to access external resources and allies to address situations.

   a. Some situations require outside resources or support. No matter how great a brain surgeon you are, you won't be very effective if you lack the proper tools, sanitary operating conditions, or other medical personnel to assist with your surgeries.

4. Does the goal support or conflict with your life purpose and highest values?

   a. For example, my value to protect my family is greater than my value to respect their privacy. This does NOT mean I randomly take liberties and invade their privacy but only do so under the extraordinary circumstances that would seriously impact their well-being.

5. The degree to which your locus of control is internal rather than externally focused.

   a. Locus of control is the degree to which we think we have some control over the events in our lives and how much is determined by external circumstances. The greater our internal locus of control, the greater our willingness to make a change.

6. The amount of consistent effort required to achieve a goal over time. The greater the amount of effort required over time, the more likely EF and your Inner Critic will make their presence known. They will work tirelessly to distract and dissuade you from committing yourself to the completion of your goals. The intensity of their efforts increases the amount of persistence needed to overcome these challenges and achieve challenging goals.

7. How well do you manage your EF?

   a. The greater the degree of EF, the more likely you are to exaggerate the effort required to achieve a goal. This impacts your locus of control and your internal conversations with your Inner Critic. When you embrace challenges that stretch without breaking you, you CAN lower your EF and increases your tolerance for emotional discomfort. Exposing yourself to progressive levels of discomfort, builds emotional muscle and allows you to take even greater challenges in stride.

8. How effectively do you manage your internal conversations and push back against your Inner Critic?

   a. Your Inner Critic is determined to maintain the status quo and relegate you to a life of mediocrity as it relates to your true potential. Managing your internal conversations to engage your Inner Critic in productive ways, allows you to consider goals you'd previously considered unattainable and actually see them through to completion. It also allows you to find greater joy in their achievement.

TABLE 2a

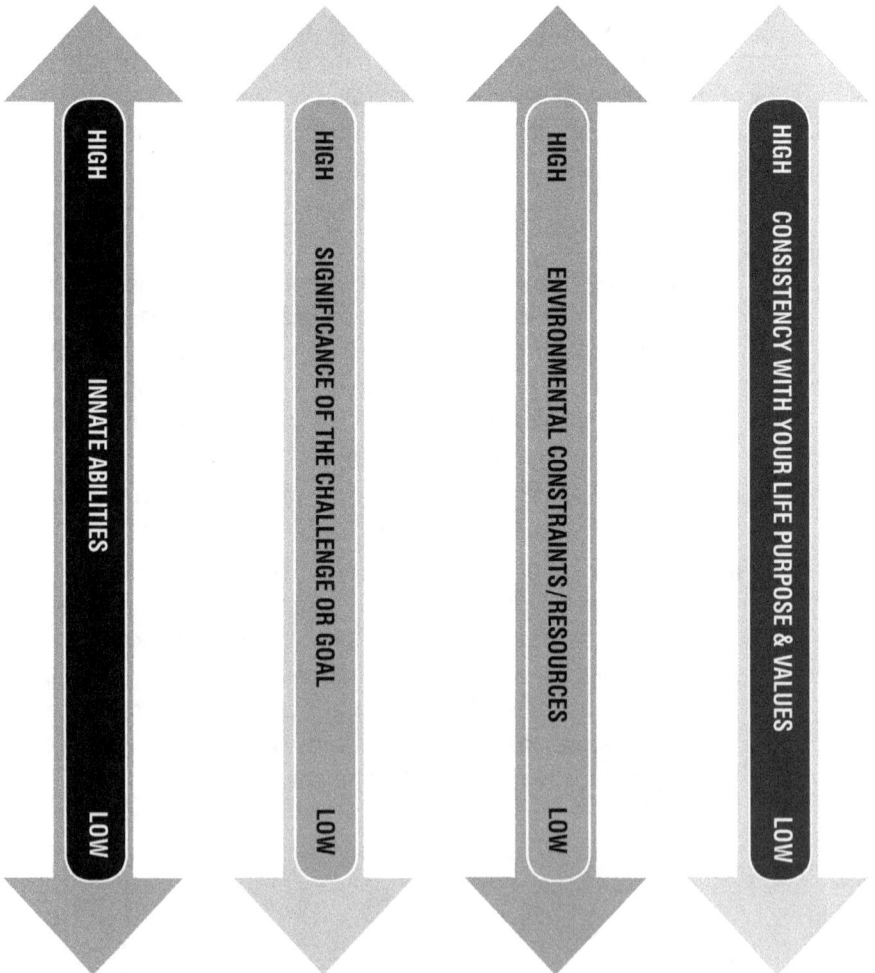

TABLE 2b

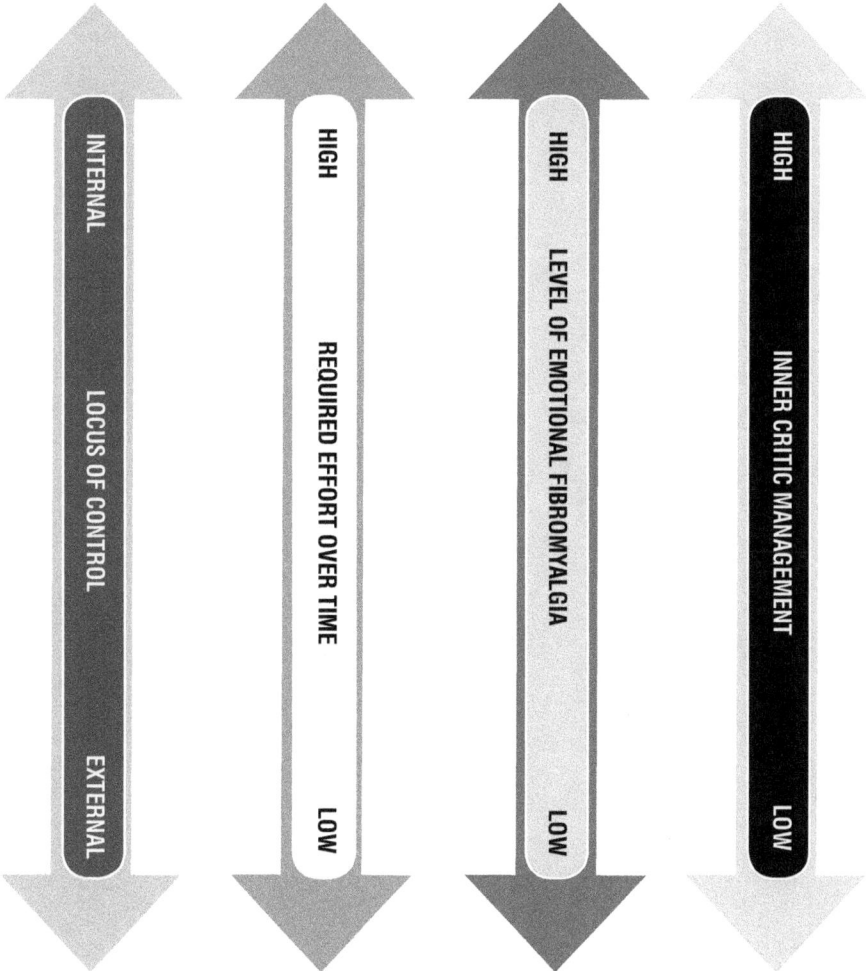

LOCUS OF CONTROL — INTERNAL / EXTERNAL

REQUIRED EFFORT OVER TIME — HIGH / LOW

LEVEL OF EMOTIONAL FIBROMYALGIA — HIGH / LOW

INNER CRITIC MANAGEMENT — HIGH / LOW

Glossary

Emotional Fibromyalgia (EF): Individuals with EF (Mild, Moderate, or Extreme have a distorted perception of their ability to tolerate emotional discomfort. They lack objective benchmarks for coping. They use their internal messaging to justify their overreactions to relatively minor events and refer to those events in hyperbolic terms.

Some individuals exhibiting signs of Moderate to Extreme forms of EF may be derisively referred to as drama queens or snowflakes. Whether they are attacked by a bear or they can't find the TV remote, their response is the same.

This does not apply to those who generally respond in measured ways and only respond in dramatic fashion when environmental circumstances call for it, such as an actual bear attack.

Fool's Errand: A task or activity that has no hope of success.

Hydra: The Hydra was a mythical serpent-like monster with many heads. If you cut off one Hydra head, two more grew back in its place.

Inner Critic: Inner Critics are sub-personalities that judge and demean us.

Intuition: Intuition is defined as the ability to understand something immediately, without the need for conscious reasoning; a thing that one knows or considers likely from instinctive feeling rather than conscious reasoning.

Machiavellian: Someone who is Machiavellian is sneaky, cunning, and lacking a moral code. The word is derived from the Italian philosopher Niccolò Machiavelli, who wrote the political treatise, "The Prince," in the 1500s. Its major tenet is that "the end justifies the means" especially among politicians.

Misapplied Strengths:	Habits that originate for a specific purpose and temporarily fulfill it. In time, the temporary benefits are far outweighed by their downsides and become Misapplied Strengths. These are often erroneously referred to as "bad habits."
Perceptual Narrowing:	Perceptual Narrowing is the tendency to restrict our focus to a single idea to the exclusion of others. This is most likely to occur during times of heightened emotional arousal.
Sirens:	Sirens are dangerous creatures in mythology who lured nearby sailors with their enchanting music and singing voices to shipwreck on the rocky coast of their island.

References

i   Conscious Competence Learning Model, Business Balls, Accessed July, 2020, http://www.businessballs.com/consciouscompetencelearn-ingmodel.htm

ii Frank Tannenbaum, Crime and the Community (New York and London: Columbia University Press.

iii Fibromyalgia, Mayo Clinic, Accessed July, 2020. https://www.mayoclinic.org/diseases-conditions/fibromyalgia/symptoms-causes/syc-20354780

iv Dina Gusovsky, "Americans Consume the Vast Majority of the World's Opiates," CNBC, Updated APR 27, 2016

v   National Institute of Health, Alcohol Facts & Statistics, Accessed July 2020. https://www.niaaa.nih.gov/publications/brochures-and-fact-sheets/alcohol-facts-and-statistics

vi H. Wechsler; G.W. Dowdall; G. Maenner; et al: "Changes in binge drinking and related problems among American college students between 1993 and 1997: Results of the Harvard School of Public Health." College Alcohol Study, Journal of American College Health 47(2):57–68, 1998. PMID: 9782661.

vii CDC, Center for Disease Control, "Underage Drinking, Consequences of Underage Drinking." Alcohol and Public Health, October, 2020.

viii Adam Tyner, Seth Gershenson, "Conceptualizing Grade Inflation" (PDF). Economics of Education Review. October 2020.

ix Gaby Gavin. The U.S. Obesity rate Now Tops 40%. U.S. News and World Report February 27, 2020, Accessed July, 2020. https://wwwusnews.com/news/healthiest-communities/articles/2020-02-27/us-obesity-rate-passes-40-percent

x   The North American Foundation for Gambling Addiction, 2016. https://nafgah.org/statistics-gambling-addiction-2016/

xi Iowa State University, Nearly 1 In 10 Youth Gamers Addicted To Video Games, Science Daily April 21, 2009.

xii Kelly Wallace, "Half of teens think they're addicted to their smartphones, CNN Health Updated, July 29, 2016.

xiii Common Sense Media, YouTube and Device Addiction, Common Sense and SurveyMonkey Poll Parents on YouTube and Technology Addiction February 22, 2018.

xiv Market Research Group Nielsen. "Time Flies: U.S. Adults Now Spend Nearly half A Day Interacting With Media," Jul 31, 2018. https://www.nielsen.com/us/en/insights/article/2018/time-flies-us-adults-now-spend-nearly-half-a-day-interacting-with-media/

www.ingramcontent.com/pod-product-compliance
Lightning Source LLC
LaVergne TN
LVHW051353080426
835509LV00020BB/3407